BRAHMS

JOHANNES BRAHMS, ÆT. 20

FROM A PENCIL DRAWING DONE FROM THE LIFE IN 1853, AT DÜSSELDORF, BY J. J. B. LAURENS, OF MONTPELLIER (1801-1890), IN THE POSSESSION OF FRAU PROFESSOR MARIA BÖIE OF BONN, BY WHOSE PERMISSION IT IS HERE REPRODUCED. THE ORIGINAL DRAWING HAS AN INSCRIPTION (PARTLY LEGIBLE IN THE REPRODUCTION,) TO THE EFFECT THAT THE DRAWING WAS DONE AT SCHUMANN'S REQUEST; THE ARTIST'S NAME IS THERE SPELT 'LAURENT,' AND THE DATE HAS BEEN ALTERED TO 1854

BRAHMS

BY

J. A. FULLER-MAITLAND

WITH TWELVE ILLUSTRATIONS

KENNIKAT PRESS
Port Washington, N. Y./London

BRAHMS

First published in 1911
Reissued in 1972 by Kennikat Press
Library of Congress Catalog Card No: 75-153898
ISBN 0-8046-1598-5

Manufactured by Taylor Publishing Company   Dallas, Texas

INTRODUCTORY NOTE ON ENTHUSIASM

THE following pages are certain to inspire distrust in the minds of some readers because of their "enthusiastic" tone. Now, although enthusiasm is no longer considered a dangerous form of insanity, as it was in the eighteenth century, yet its presence is still regarded as tending to obscure the judgment, and the word conveys, whether intentionally or not, some idea of a mood that is necessarily transitory. The lamp that is trimmed gives the brightest and purest light, and the very sound of "enthusiasm" suggests some of the unpleasant accompaniments of an untrimmed wick. But is "enthusiasm" rightly predicted of all eulogy? Is all eulogy to be distrusted on the ground that no opinion can be at once favourable and dispassionate? One sees how absurd the word sounds in regard to the supreme things of the world in art and literature. Enthusiasm about the Bible, Shakespeare, Dante, Michel Angelo, or Beethoven savours of a young ladies' seminary, and in a grown-up person is as unfitting on the one hand as "impartial" criticism would be on the other, although in the days shortly following the creation of the supreme things, enthusiasm and impartiality were quite appropriately exhibited towards them. Surely a frame of mind exists in which admiration for the greatest things is unmixed with any restless anxiety to discover flaws, a frame of mind free from all feverish desire to "gush" over things which, having attained the position of classics, remain for the world's calm and steady delight. Perhaps the most recent of the incontestably supreme things in the world of music to call forth a display of "impartiality" was the life-work of Beethoven, upon whose death there were written obituary notices which must amuse the modern critic, and should warn him against a timid excess of coolness. The fact that the tone of many of the obituary notices of Brahms was unwittingly couched in the same kind of "temperate" language would of itself suggest the idea that that master's work was destined to rank among the great things of the world. It may be well to make it clear that the following pages are not written with any desire to make unwilling converts, but to explain the writer's own personal conviction regarding the music of Brahms. For him it has always been difficult to get into the position of a person who finds Brahms puzzling or crabbed; from the date of the early performances of the first sextet at the Popular Concerts the master's ways of expressing himself, his idioms, have always seemed the most natural and gracious that could be conceived. Not that any unusual degree of musical insight can be claimed, nor any desire felt to disguise the few occasions on which passages have not been absolutely clear at a first hearing; but it would be hardly honest to disarm criticism by adopting an artificial "impartiality" when the joy aroused by that first experience has spread and grown with unwavering steadiness for over thirty years, during which each new work, as it appeared, has been eagerly welcomed as a new revelation of a spirit already ardently loved. It may be remarked that on that first occasion of encountering the name of Brahms on a concert programme, the music was allowed to make its own impression. Musically inclined elders, anxious to train the young in the orthodox ways, as orthodoxy was understood in the seventies, were accustomed, with the best intentions, to call Handel sublime, Bach dry, Mozart shallow, and Mendelssohn sweet; of Beethoven they spoke in tones that reminded the child of Sunday, telling him he could not expect to understand it till he was older, or to enjoy it till much later; thus, all unconsciously, they damped for many years any ardour he might have felt for the great masters. But Brahms was a new name and could not be "placed"; so that at once and for ever afterwards he seemed to speak to the heart with a rare directness, to use phrases that seemed to come from the home of the soul, and to speak so intimately as even to destroy any wish for personal communication with the man lest that might perchance detract from the eloquence of his music.

J. A. FULLER-MAITLAND

CONTENTS

LIST OF ILLUSTRATIONS

BRAHMS

CHAPTER I

BIOGRAPHICAL

THE advantages of an uneventful life, so obvious in the case of the happy nations that have no history, are less patent in regard to artistic careers. Goethe's "Wer nie sein Brod mit Thränen ass" is one of the most hackneyed quotations in existence, and is always brought forward to prove the great benefit resulting from personal affliction upon the minds of those who deal with the arts. It is so easy to show by its means that one man must have been an excellent painter because he could not get on with his wife, another a fine poet because he committed suicide, or that the operas of a third must be of excellent quality because the composer forged a banknote. Had Beethoven been the uncle of a respectable nephew instead of a hopeless ne'er-do-weel, had Wagner prolonged his wedded life and not meddled with politics, had Schubert been rich instead of poor, had Handel kept his eyesight, we may be sure that certain writers of the present day would have been found to place them, on this account, among the composers of whom Mendelssohn is the popular type, with his unfailing outward prosperity and his frequent lapses from musical greatness. We may admit that the indigestible character of modern Russian food has had much to do with the pessimism of modern Russian music; but the bread of tears is seldom made of flour, and many a great man has eaten it whose outward life seems to have passed in an unruffled calm, and whose biographer is at his wits' end to find some stain on his reputation, some skeleton in the cupboard to be brought forth as evidence of his close intimacy with the "heavenly powers." These skeletons do undoubtedly serve the purpose of awakening interest in the work of the owners of their cupboards; and the public vogue of a man with whom scandal has been busy is naturally greater than that of one against whose conduct nothing can be adduced. If a man's work declare itself as of supreme quality throughout, and prove that he has been "commercing with the skies," we are surely permitted to regard him as a rare exception to Goethe's rule, or to admit the possibility that his sorrows may have been real enough, even though they were hidden from the keenest human eye. A man's creations are far surer evidence of his emotional range than any list of social upheavals, personal privations, or scandalous actions; and while those whose being vibrates to every characteristic mood of a musician's art need no outside testimony to his greatness, the less fortunate persons to whom that art is a sealed book are not likely to be convinced of its importance by a categorical account of the sorrows the musician endured.

Such an outwardly uneventful life was that of Johannes Brahms, and it is only necessary to give a rapid summary of the main facts, pointing out the few incidents which bear directly upon his music. He was the second child and elder son of Johann Jakob Brahms and his wife, Johanna Henrika Christiana Nissen, who were married in 1830 and lived in humble circumstances in part of a large house, No. 60, Speckstrasse, Hamburg.[1] The father, who had studied various stringed instruments and the flute, was a horn-player in the Bürger-Militair, or town-guard of Hamburg, and afterwards a double-bass player in a regular string band; the mother, described as a small, plain, limping woman of delicate health and sensitive disposition, seems to have had few accomplishments except that of being a good needle-woman. Johannes Brahms was born on 7 May, 1833, and baptized on the 26th at St. Michael's Church. A pianist named Cossel, a pupil of Eduard Marxsen of Altona, taught the boy the piano from the time he was seven years old, and it was due to this man's perseverance that, after several refusals, Marxsen himself consented to take him as a pupil, at first for piano only. He played a study of Herz at a charity concert when he was ten years old. When he was fourteen, one Adolph Giesemann, a frequent attendant at the performances of the band of which Jakob Brahms was a member, consented to take the boy into the country for a change, to Winsen-an-der-Luhe; here he went on with his music, teaching Herr Giesemann's little daughter, and travelling every week to Altona for his lesson with Marxsen. He conducted a small choir of male voices at Winsen, and composed a few pieces for its use. In November, 1847, he appeared at public concerts in Hamburg, on the 20th and 27th, playing at his first appearance Thalberg's

[1] A photograph of the house is to be found in Miss May's *Life oj Brahms*, i. 52.

Norma fantasia, and at the second a duet by the same popular virtuoso with Frau Meyer-David, the concert-giver. Nearly a year afterwards, on 21 September, 1848, he gave a concert of his own, at which he played a fugue of Bach, besides other things more suited to the taste of that day. On 14 April, 1849, he gave another concert, playing the "Waldstein" sonata of Beethoven, some popular pieces, and a fantasia by himself "on a favourite waltz." After this formal opening of his career as an executant, he had to endure the drudgery of playing night after night in dancing saloons. During the next five years his life must have been a hard one, and perhaps some of the necessary bread of tears was eaten at this time. Various small engagements, one of which was that of accompanist behind the scenes of the Stadt Theater, and teaching (at the high fee of about a shilling a lesson) occupied him, and in his spare time he read voraciously, poetry turning itself, half consciously, into music in his brain. Many songs were composed at this period of his life, when he was compelled, like Wagner, to do hack-work for publishers in the way of arrangements and transcriptions, operatic and otherwise; these were published under the pseudonym of "G. W. Marks," and it would seem as though another *nom de plume*, "Karl Würth," was kept for work of a more ambitious kind, such as duet for piano and violoncello, and a trio for piano and strings, which were played at a private concert on 5 July, 1851, and duly announced on the programme as the work of "Karl Würth"; a copy of the programme is still in existence on which Brahms has substituted in pencil his true name for the other.

Not till 1853 did a brighter day dawn for the composer. A certain violinist named Reményi, whose real name was Hoffmann, and who was of a mixed German, Hungarian, and Jewish origin, had appeared in Hamburg as early as 1849, ostensibly on his way to America with other Hungarian refugees. He found the "farewell" concert as profitable as numberless English artists have found it at various times, and after the departure of his compatriots for the United States he still lingered on in Hamburg until 1851. He then seems to have gone to America for a time, but he reappeared, at first in Paris, in 1852, and at Hamburg again in the winter of 1852–3. It was arranged that Brahms should act as his accompanist at three concerts, at Winsen, Lüneburg, and Celle, and finally should proceed thence to Hanover, where Joachim was court concertmeister (*i.e.*, leader of the band), and assistant capellmeister (conductor), having given up his position as leader of the opera orchestra. The number of concerts was extended to about seven in all, at which the same programme was gone through by the two performers. Beethoven's sonata in C minor from Op. 30 was the most important composition performed. At Celle, where the only decent piano was a semitone too low for the violinist's convenience, Brahms undertook to play the sonata in C sharp minor, at a moment's notice. Reményi was not a great artist, and would be of small importance in the career of Brahms if he had not happened to be slightly acquainted with Joachim.

The meeting between Joachim and Brahms, which was the beginning of a lifelong and most fruitful intimacy, took place at Joachim's rooms in Hanover,[1] and it was obvious to the older man that Brahms was no ordinary musician. In the oration pronounced by Joachim at the dedication of the Brahms monument at Meiningen,

[1] See Miss May's *Life*, i. 106, note.

7 October, 1899, this first meeting is thus referred to: "It was a revelation to me when the song *O versenk'* struck my ears. And his piano-playing besides was so tender, so full of fancy, so free, so fiery, that it held me enthralled." After hearing such compositions as the young composer had brought with him, which included various movements of sonatas, the scherzo Op. 4, a sonata for piano and violin, a trio, and a string quartet, beside several songs, Joachim saw plainly that the association with a performer of Reményi's stamp was not likely to be a lasting one, and he invited Brahms to visit him at Göttingen (where he—Joachim—was about to attend lectures) in the event of his tiring of his present post. There was some discussion between the two as to the order in which it would be advisable to publish Brahms's early compositions.[1] At the time Joachim could do no more than give Brahms a letter of introduction to Liszt, as the pair of players intended to go to Weimar. The account of the interview with Liszt, given by William Mason, who was present, may be read in Miss May's *Life*.[2] That Liszt played at sight the scherzo and approved of its style, is the one fact that is really important; it is curious to read that after Raff had detected its (very obvious) likeness to Chopin's pieces in the same form, Brahms assured a friend that he had no knowledge whatever of the Polish master's scherzos. The reception of the two players by Liszt was of the most cordial, and they found, what so many others found before and afterwards, an atmosphere of flattering appreciation, practical kindness, and surroundings which could not but appeal to any ardent and artistic soul. It was Liszt's way to express to the full all the admiration he felt, but on

[1] See the *Joachim Correspondence*, i. 10–12. [2] Vol. i. 110.

BRAHMS AND REMENYI

this occasion a letter of his to Bülow [1] proves that he really thought highly of the C major sonata. For six [2] weeks the fellow-travellers stayed at Weimar, but gradually it became clear to Brahms at least that the spell of Armida's garden must be resisted, and every night when he went to bed he resolved to cut the visit short, but every morning a new enchantment seemed to be put upon him, and he stayed. The charm was broken almost as effectually as that of Venus in *Tannhäuser*, but in a less poetical manner. William Mason tells us in his *Memories of a Musical Life* that Liszt was on one occasion playing his beloved sonata in B minor, and, glancing round at a very expressive moment of the piece, saw that Brahms was slumbering peacefully; the composer stopped abruptly and left the room. The figure of Reményi goes out of the story; his political and musical proclivities continued to appeal to Liszt, and in the year after he was made violinist to Queen Victoria. Although armed with Joachim's letter, Brahms hesitated for some little time before presenting himself to Schumann at Düsseldorf. Steeped in the classical traditions he had learnt from Marxsen, he had been almost deaf to the appeal of Schumann's music, for which a great friend, Fräulein Louise Japha, had unbounded admiration. Brahms had sent Schumann a number of his early compositions in 1850, when Schumann was at Hamburg; but the older master was then too busy to open the parcel. When he did make up his mind to go over from Mehlem, where he had been staying almost ever since his departure from Weimar, he was welcomed at once by the Schumanns, whose expectations had been aroused by Joachim. When Brahms sat

[1] *Franz Liszt*, von Julius Kapp, p. 281.

[2] According to Kapp, p. 280; Kalbeck says the time was three weeks.

down to the piano to play one of his compositions to Schumann, the latter interrupted him with the words, "Clara must hear this," and he told his wife, when she came into the room, "Here, dear Clara, you will hear such music as you never heard before; now, begin again, young man!" They kept Brahms to dinner, and received him into their intimacy.[1] To Joachim Schumann wrote the memorable words, "This is he that should come"—words which, with the equally famous article, *Neue Bahnen*, claimed for Brahms a place in the royal succession of the great German composers. The article was all the more powerful since Schumann broke in it his four years' silence as a critic. It was not an altogether unqualified benefit to Brahms, seeing that it naturally aroused much antagonism both among the many musicians who did not yet know Brahms's compositions, and also among the few who, knowing them, did not like them. In October, 1853, Brahms collaborated with Schumann and Albert Dietrich in the composition of a sonata for piano and violin as a present of welcome to Joachim, who visited Düsseldorf. The first movement, by Dietrich, and the intermezzo and finale by Schumann, have not been published, as Joachim, who possessed the autograph, considered the latter master's contribution not to be quite worthy of him, and to show signs of the mental ailment which was so soon to overshadow him; but he gave permission for the publication, after Brahms's death, of the scherzo in C minor, which was the youngest man's share. Later in the same year came a visit to Leipzig, and an appearance at the Gewandhaus, at one of David's quartet-concerts, in which Brahms played his own C major sonata

[1] Dr. A. Schubring's *Schumanniana*, quoted by Kalbeck, *Johannes Brahms*, i. 121.

and the E flat minor scherzo. At this time, too, occurred the last attempt of the "advanced" school to induce Brahms to return to the ranks of Liszt's followers; Liszt was in Leipzig, in order to be present when Berlioz conducted important compositions at the Gewandhaus. Brahms found Liszt quite inclined to let bygones be bygones, and Berlioz was heard to praise the young artist (whether as performer or composer we are not told).[1] By this time there was, of course, little hope that the fixed convictions of Brahms would be unsettled, and personal as well as artistic reasons must have weighed with him against any real reconciliation with the Liszt school. He took up his residence at Hanover in order to work hard in congenial surroundings, and for the sake of the constant intercourse with Joachim. There, too, he saw Schumann again, for the last time before the tragic attempt at suicide. Schumann had come to Hanover for a performance of his *Paradise and the Peri*, and enjoyed the society of Joachim, Brahms, and Julius Otto Grimm. From the sad event of 27 February, when Schumann threw himself into the Rhine, Joachim and Brahms stood in a position of a filial or fraternal kind to Madame Schumann, who, throughout all her anxieties, bravely followed her artistic career in spite of the additional distress caused by her not being allowed to see her afflicted husband. The variations of Brahms on a theme by Schumann, in F sharp minor, Op. 9, are lasting evidence of the close intimacy which was only terminated by death. The variations, and the next compositions, the four *Balladen*, Op. 10, gave the greatest pleasure to Schumann.

In 1855 there was some talk of Brahms being appointed to the post that Schumann had held in Düsseldorf, but it was

[1] Kalbeck, *op. cit.*, i. 148.

felt that, standing as he had done in a relation of peculiar intimacy with Schumann, he could not enter as a candidate for the post, which was given to Julius Tausch in due course.

In 1856, after Schumann's death, Brahms arranged to relieve Madame Schumann of some of the lessons she was engaged to give, and among the pupils was a Fräulein Laura von Meysenbug, whose father and brother were officials at the court of Lippe-Detmold, and whose mother was an accomplished amateur pianist. Princess Friederike of Lippe-Detmold was another of Madame Schumann's pupils, and in consequence of the connection thus formed, Brahms was offered a kind of informal appointment at the court of Detmold, where he was to conduct a choral society recently re-organized, to perform at the court concerts, and to continue the Princess's musical education. His duties only lasted through the winter season, from September to December, and he gained much useful experience as a conductor during the two years of his engagement at the court, which he retained until January, 1860. About this time he made the acquaintance of a young Göttingen lady, Fräulein Agathe von Siebold, with whom he seems to have fallen in love; there are various signs that it was a serious passion on his part, but worldly considerations made a marriage out of the question, and the fact that in his G major sextet there occurs this theme in the first movement is the most important record of the episode.[1]

In 1859 the first performance of the D minor concerto for pianoforte, with the composer in the solo

[1] See Litzmann's *Clara Schumann*, iii. 70.

part, took place at Hanover, Leipzig, and Hamburg, being received at the first two very coldly. At the Gewandhaus of Leipzig its reception was distinctly unfavourable ; but Brahms took his repulse philosophically, and in a letter to Joachim (who had conducted it at Hanover) he says: "I believe it is the best thing that could happen to me ; for it compels one to order one's thoughts and to pluck up courage for the future." It is perhaps significant that the loudest notes of disapproval were from the extreme classicists of Leipzig ; the partisans of the new school of Weimar found more in it to praise, and it is greatly to their credit that they had the courage to say so. It has been suggested that this praise was bestowed as part of a deliberate plan to get hold of Brahms's allegiance to the new school and its tenets ; but whether it was so or not, the event showed that his devotion to the classical models had undergone no change. Brahms's position in regard to the new school was settled once for all by an awkward accident. In 1860, it had been given out in the *Neue Zeitschrift für Musik*, the organ of the new school, that all the most prominent musicians of the day were in favour of the "music of the future," as it was called. Brahms felt it to be his duty to protest against this falsehood, and consented to sign a document expressing disapproval of the high-handed and wholly gratuitous assumption ; the *Erklärung* seems to have been written by Joachim and Bernhard Scholz, and a great number of influential musicians undertook to subscribe it, but while it was actually going round for signatures, a version of it got into print in the Berlin *Echo*, with only four names appended to it ; that those of Brahms and Joachim were among the

[1] See *Joachim Correspondence*, i. 227–9.

four was, of course, not forgotten nor forgiven by the Weimar partisans.[1]

The text of the famous "Declaration" may be thus translated: —

The undersigned have for some time followed with regret the course pursued by a certain party, whose organ is Brendel's *Zeitschrift für Musik.*

The said *Zeitschrift* gives wide publicity to the opinion that musicians of earnest aims are in agreement with the tendencies followed by the paper, and recognize in the compositions of the leaders of the movement works of artistic value, and that the dispute as to the so-called "Music of the Future" has been already fought out, particularly in North Germany, and decided in favour of the movement.

The undersigned consider it their duty to protest against such a misstatement of facts, and to declare for their part at least that they do not recognize the principles expressed in Brendel's *Zeitschrift*, and that they can only bewail or condemn, as against the inmost and essential nature of music, the productions of the leaders and pupils of the so-called "New German" school, which on the one hand give practical expression to these principles, and on the other necessitate the establishment of new and unheard-of theories.

JOHANNES BRAHMS.
JOSEPH JOACHIM.
JULIUS OTTO GRIMM.
BERNHARD SCHOLZ.

[1] On the whole question of the letter, and Brahms's attitude towards it, see the *Joachim Correspondence*, i. 257, 268–9, 274, 279. Also Kalbeck, i. chap. x.

This was accompanied by the following letter to those who were invited to add their names:—

We feel that all to whom this is presented for signature may wish to add much to this declaration; as we believe that each of them is in perfect agreement with the sense of the foregoing, we beg them earnestly to reflect on the importance of not putting aside the protest, and we have therefore tried to simplify the above document sent for signature. In case you are willing to associate yourself with us, we ask you to send in this page, duly signed, to Herr Johannes Brahms, Hohe Fuhlentwiete 74, Hamburg. The declaration with the names in alphabetical order will be published in the musical periodicals.

The above signatories.

It is obvious that every additional name would have added greatly to the effect of this document, which may or may not have been a very politic one; but with only four names, although these included two of the most prominent of the German classicists, it could not but excite derision, and foster the inimical feelings of the men at whom it was directed. It was, as we can all see now, an expedient of no practical utility whatever; but there are moments when it is beyond human power to resist the temptation to nail to the counter such lies as had been uttered in the newspaper. Music, surely more than the other arts, has been liable to these outbursts of personal feeling, and every artistic revolution in its history must have stirred up recriminations of one kind or another. Happily we do not know exactly in what terms Palestrina and the masters of the polyphonic school of the sixteenth century were attacked by the men who strove for some new means of expression. We know a good deal more about the war of the Gluckists and Piccinnists in Paris, and more still about the silly rivalry between popular singers in the period of Handelian operas in London. In Germany the lovers of music are always curiously apt to take sides and split into two opposing parties, and it is easy to see that in many cases there is a good deal of reason on both sides. The classical party, whether itself creative or not, must feel responsible for the handing down of a great tradition in its purity, and that it should exaggerate the iconoclastic intentions of the other side is perhaps inevitable ; the party identified with tendencies that are new will, of course, secure the approval of the majority ; and, while always ready enough to pose as martyrs for truths that have been revealed to them alone, will as certainly minimize any originality which the works of the classicists may display. We know now that the "Declaration" was not a protest by hide-bound pedants against all the modern tendencies, but was really directed against special heresies which were traced in some of Liszt's Symphonic Poems. Brahms, as appears from his correspondence with Joachim,[1] was particularly anxious not to include the music of Wagner in his condemnation of the modern tendencies, and it must not be forgotten that the friends did not take the initiative in the matter, but were bound to traverse the implied statement that all the eminent musicians of Germany were on the one side. While we know that the classical forms seemed to him sacred, yet on occasion he found it expedient to modify them in various ways, not from any poverty of his own ideas, but as it were to encourage the natural development of a living organism. The "new school," for whose thoughts the older forms were

[1] i. 274.

too scanty or too strictly defined, did, after all, very little indeed towards any really fruitful development of musical form, and it is hard to get rid of the suspicion that the older forms were thrown aside by their leader on account of the easily recognized difficulties they present to one whose musical ideas are virtually without distinction. It is idle to guess what might have been the state of musical parties in Germany at the present day if the Weimar school had confined themselves to the accurate statement that a large number of musicians had embraced their principles; but it is hardly probable that any degree of personal or artistic intimacy could ever have endured between men whose constitutional modesty made them hate all that was tawdry, and those to whom the adulation of a large public was as the breath of their nostrils, and who cared little for the real merits of their music as long as it was likely to surprise or tickle the ears of their audiences.

Liszt's admirable breadth of view, his boundless generosity towards musicians of every kind, and his surpassing genius as an executant, must have counted for very much in his own day; but there is no gainsaying the fact that adoption of his methods of composition and of artistic ideals based upon his, has brought German music into a most singular state at the present time. It is clear that Brendel himself thought he had gone rather too far in support of the Weimar clique; for he afterwards allowed Schubring to express his convictions that Brahms was one of the giants of music, a man on the level of Bach, Beethoven, and Schumann, and had to make his peace with the "new" composers as best he might in a "hedging" article,[1] in which he makes a somewhat ludicrous attempt to run with the hare and hunt with the

[1] Kalbeck, i. 490.

hounds. The extraordinary warmth of feeling exhibited by the new school after the "Declaration" and after the memorable letter written by Joachim to Liszt [1] has been, no doubt rightly, ascribed to the great influence wielded by Joachim, and in a lesser degree by Brahms. Had the "New School" realized how many and how influential were the names that would have appeared below the "Declaration" if its appearance had not been forestalled, it is at least possible that their resentment would not have been so exclusively against Brahms and Joachim; and it is even possible that Wagner's famous *Judenthum in der Musik*, the pamphlet which rendered any idea of reconciliation for ever impossible, might never have been written. The names of those who had promised to support the "Declaration" are referred to in the letters between Joachim and Brahms, but it does not appear that they were made in any way public before the issue of the correspondence in 1908.

At Hamburg Brahms was busily and congenially occupied as conductor of a choir of ladies, on whose behalf he wrote the various sacred and secular works for female voices which are so numerous among his early opus-numbers. Many more were written, but were burnt by the composer, all but a single part (second soprano), in which Kalbeck discovered the germs of several mature works.[2] The choir was developed from the fortuitous association of some ladies in the music arranged by Grädener for the marriage of a pastor named Sengelmann with a Fräulein Jenny von Ahsen. Brahms played the organ at the ceremony, and Grädener composed a motet for female voices, the effect of which was so good, that

[1] Moser's *Joseph Joachim*, p. 151. English translation, p. 167.
[2] i. pp. 277, 386.

Brahms asked the ladies to study his own *Ave Maria* and two other choral works for the same voices; gradually a regular choral society was founded and the work of conducting it and writing music for it gave Brahms yet more experience in practical music. The details of the society, with various reminiscences of members, etc., may be read in the *Jahrbuch* of the Gesellschaft Hamburgischer Kunstfreunde for 1902, where Frau Lentz, geb. Meier, writes a series of *Brahms-Erinnerungen*. These are largely quoted by Kalbeck, who gives a full account of the society in his *Life*.[1]

An amusing code of rules for the society was drawn up by Brahms for the use of the ladies in the queer bilingual style with which readers of Mattheson and the eighteenth-century German writers are familiar. The document is so amusing an illustration of Brahms's characteristic humour that it seems worth while to quote it entire:—

"AVERTIMENTO

"Sonder weilen es *absolute* dem *Plaisire* fördersam ist, wenn es fein ordentlich dabei einhergeht, als wird denen *curieusen* Gemüthern, so Mitglieder des sehr nutz- und lieblichen *Frauenchors* wünschen zu werden und zu bleiben jetzund kund und offenbar gethan, dass sie *partoute* die *Clausuln* und *Puncti* hiefolgenden Geschreibsels unter zu zeichnen haben, ehe sie sich obgenannten *Tituls* erfreuen und an der musikalischen Erlustigung und *Divertierung parte* nehmen können.

"Ich hätte zwaren schon längst damit unter der Bank herfür wischen sollen, alleine aberst dennoch, weilen der Frühling erst lieblich *präambuliret* und bis der Sommer

[1] i. 367 ff.

finiret, gesungen werden dürfte, als möchte es noch an der Zeit sein dieses *Opus* an das Tageslicht zu stellen.

"*Pro primo* wäre zu remarquiren dass die Mitglieder des *Frauenchors* d a sein müssen.

"Als wird verstanden; dass sie sich *obligiren* sollen, den Stehungen und Singungen der *Societät* regelmässig beizuwohnen.

"So nun Jemand diesen *Articul* nicht gehörig *observiret* und, wo Gott für sei, der Fall *passirete*, dass Jemand wider jedes *Decorum* so fehlete, dass er während eines *Exercitiums* ganz fehlete;

"soll gestraft werden mit einer Busse von 8 Schillingen H.C. (Hamburger Courant).

"*Pro secundo* ist zu beachten, dass die Mitglieder des Frauenchors d a sein müssen.

"Als ist zu nehmen, sie sollen *praecise* zur anberaumten Zeit da sein.

"Wer nun hiewieder also sündiget, dass er das ganze Viertheil einer Stunde zu spät der *Societät* seine schuldige *Reverentz* und Aufwartung machet, soll um 2 Schillinge H.C. gestrafet werden.

("Ihrer grossen *Meriten* um den *Frauenchor* wegen und in Betracht ihrer vermuthlich höchst mangelhaften und unglücklichen *Complexion*, soll nun hier für die nicht genug zu *favorirende* und *adorirende Demoiselle Laura Garbe* ein *Abonnement* hergestellt werden, wesmassen sie nicht jedesmal zu bezahlen braucht, sondern aber ihro am Schluss des Quartals eine *moderirte* Rechnung praesentiret wird):

"*Pro tertio:* Das einkommende Geld mag denen Bettelleuten gegeben werden und wird gewünscht, dass Niemand davon gesättiget werden möge.

"*Pro quarto* ist zu merken, dass die *Musikalien* grossentheils der *Discretion* der *Dames* anvertrauet sind. Derohalben sollen sie wie fremdes Eigenthum von den ehr- und tugendsamen Jungfrauen und Frauen in rechter Lieb und aller Hübschheit gehalten werden, auch in keinerlei Weise ausserhalb der *Societät* werden.

"*Pro quinto:* Was nicht mit singen kann, das sehen wir als ein *Neutrum* an. Will heissen: Zuhörer werden geduldet indessen aber *pro ordinario* beachtet, was Gestalt sonsten die rechte Nutzbarkeit der *Exercitia* nicht beschaffet werden möchte.

"Obgemeldeter gehörig *specifizirter* Erlass wird durch gegenwärtiges *General-Rescript* anjetzo jeder männiglich *public* gemacht und soll in Würden gehalten werden, bis der *Frauenchor* seine Endschaft erreichet hat.

"Solltest du nun nicht nur vor dich ohnverbrüchlich darob halten, sondern auch alles Ernstes daran sein, dass andere auf keinerlei Weise noch Wege darwider thun noch handeln mögen.

"An dem beschiehet Unsere Meinung und erwarte *aero* gewünschte und wohlgewogene *Approbation.*

"Der ich verharre in tiefster *Devotion* und *Veneration* des Frauenchors allzeit dienstbeflissener schreibfertiger und taktfester

"JOHANNES KREISLER, JUN.,
"*alias:* BRAHMS

"Geben auf Montag,
"den 30ten. des *Monats Aprili.*
"A.D. 1860."[1]

It is far from easy to convey the exact meaning of the quaint old-world language, and to render it by any adequate

[1] The words in italics appear in Roman type in Kalbeck's *Life*, the rest being in German character.

English equivalent seems quite impossible; the following translation aims at nothing more than giving the general drift of the document:—

AVERTIMENTO

Inasmuch as it is an undoubted enhancement of pleasure that it should be well-regulated and in order, it is hereby declared and made plain to those inquiring spirits who wish to become members of the very useful and lovely Ladies' Choir, that they must sign the whole of the clauses and periods of the here-following script, before they can enjoy the above title and take part in the musical enjoyment and diversion.

I ought to have got the thing started before now,[1] but (from) the advent of lovely spring until the end of summer, is a season proclaimed as the most fitting for singing, and the time is ripe for the execution of the scheme.

In the first place, it is to be noticed that the members of the Ladies' Choir are to be *there*.

That is to say: they shall undertake to attend regularly the meetings and practices of the Society.

If any one shall not observe this condition, and if the case should happen (which Heaven forfend!) that any one should so err against decorum as to miss a whole practice;

[1] The meaning of the phrase "unter der Bank wischen" is clearly "to sweep under the bench," but it is difficult to be sure in what sense the phrase is used. On the one hand, it has been suggested that it refers (as a phrase usual in Hamburg houses) to the periodical "spring cleaning," but it is more probable (considering the legal character of the whole document) that the "Bank" referred to is the "lange Bank," or shelf, on which deeds were placed in rows, those not immediately wanted being pushed along it, so that "to shove anything along the long shelf" means to postpone it indefinitely. Conversely, in the above, "I should have swept it out from under the shelf" may bear the meaning suggested in the text, but the general gist of the paragraph is clearly to confine the choral practices to the spring and summer.

she shall be mulcted in a fine of 8 shillings (Hamburg currency).

In the second place, it is to be noticed, that the members of the Ladies' Choir are to be there.

That is to say, they shall be punctual to the appointed time.

If any one so transgresses as to be a whole quarter of an hour too late in paying his due respect and attendance to the Society, he shall be fined 2 shillings (Hamburg currency).

(On account of her great merit in regard to the choir, and in respect of her probably highly faulty and unfortunate [delicacy of] constitution, a subscription shall be got up for the never-enough-to-be-favoured-and-adored Demoiselle Laura Garbe, so that she need not pay every time [that she is absent or late], but that a reduced account shall be presented to her at the end of the quarter.)

In the third place, the money so collected may be given to the poor, and it is hoped that none of them will be surfeited therewith.

In the fourth place, it is to be noticed, that the music is for the most part confided to the discretion of the ladies. Therefore the honourable and virtuous ladies, married or single, shall preserve it neatly and fairly, like the property of some one else, and it is by no means to go outside the society.

In the fifth place: Whatsoever cannot sing with us, we regard as of the neuter gender. That is to say, Listeners are tolerated, only so far as they do nothing that could interfere with the practical utility of the practices.

The above permission is definitely made by the present document, and shall be observed by each and all of the public, until the Ladies' Choir shall come to an end.

You shall not only comply with this without fail, but shall do your best endeavour to prevent others from disobeying the rules.

To whom our decisions are submitted [?] and whose desired and well-weighed approval is awaited in deepest devotion and veneration; by the Ladies' Choir's diligent ready-writer and time-beater,

JOHANNES KREISLER, JUN.,
alias BRAHMS

It is not surprising to hear that the joke about Demoiselle Garbe and her frequent unpunctuality was not especially pleasing to the poor lady, who consulted Frau Schumann about it. That lady, who was one of those who signed the document as being a member of the Ladies' Choir, pointed out that in such a document as this her name would be handed down to posterity. It all seems a little childish, and the whole business of the rules has, of course, lost a good deal of what point it ever had, but it seems worth preserving for its quaint phraseology. Frau Schumann's presence in Hamburg at the date of the document is denied by Miss May,[1] but Kalbeck says that she played on 20 April, ten days before the above date, at a concert of Otten's Musical Society, at which Brahms repeated the solo part in his ill-fated concerto. It was awkwardly placed in the programme, and the reception of the first movement was so unfavourable that the composer got up and whispered to Otten, the conductor, that he must decline to go on with the work. Happily Otten persuaded him to finish it. The episode has nothing in itself remarkable, but in regard to the failure of this work here and in Leipzig, we are in danger of forgetting that

[1] *Life*, i. 254.

Brahms's stoical manner was only assumed, and here we see how sorely he felt the attitude of the public. It may or may not have had to do with the composer's slowly formed determination to go and live in Vienna, which he visited in 1862, apparently meaning to remain only a short time.

The migration from Hamburg and the ultimate adoption of Vienna as a home, is generally and conveniently held to mark the principal division in the outward career of Brahms. An appointment to the conductorship of the Vienna Singakademie was perhaps the immediate cause of the change of abode, and although the office was only retained for a year or two, yet, by the time Brahms gave it up, Vienna had become so attractive to him that he made it his head-quarters for the rest of his life. The conception and completion of his great *Deutsches Requiem* occupied him chiefly for the next five years or so. Not that his labours in other fields were unimportant, for the compositions of the early Viennese period include his two most exacting pianoforte solos, the "Handel" and "Paganini" variations, the two quartets for piano and strings, Opp. 25 and 26, the quintet in F minor, Op. 34, the *Magelone* romances, and many other vocal works. It is, happily, unnecessary for the ordinary lover of Brahms's *Requiem* to settle definitely whether it was intended to enshrine the memory of the composer's mother (a theory supported by the disposition of the fifth section, the famous soprano solo and chorus, and by the direct testimony of Joachim and other friends), or whether it was, as strenuously argued by Herr Kalbeck, suggested by the tragedy of Schumann's end. Possibly both are in a measure true; the composer may have been first led to meditate on death and its problems by the death of Schumann—the first deep personal sorrow he can have known—but we know that in chronological sequence its composition followed his own private loss. Frau Brahms died in 1865, and the *Requiem* was completed in 1868 by the addition of the number already referred to. Before the performance of the first three numbers (1867), the widower had married again, and there are few things more beautiful in Brahms's life than his conduct to his stepmother, over whose interests, and those of her son by a former marriage, Fritz Schnack, he watched with rare loyalty. His father died in 1872, Frau Caroline Brahms surviving her illustrious stepson by five years. About the period of the *Requiem*, or rather later, came several other works in which a chorus takes part, such as *Rinaldo*, for male voices, and three of the noblest choral compositions in existence: the *Rhapsodie*, for contralto solo, male choir, and orchestra; the *Schicksalslied* and *Triumphlied*, the last, in eight parts, with solo for bass, in commemoration of the German victories in the war of 1870–1. For three seasons, 1872–5, Brahms was conductor of the concerts of the Gesellschaft der Musikfreunde, and the programmes of the period given in Miss May's *Life* are enough to fill us with envy. During this time his music was continually advancing in popularity, and the great public of Vienna was conquered by the remarkable performance of the *Requiem* there on 28 February, 1875. This new attitude of the public gave the cue to the rest of the world, and during a tour in Holland in 1876 even the D minor concerto roused enthusiasm when the composer played it at Utrecht. The "Haydn" variations for orchestra were given in various musical centres, always with great success, but it was the first symphony, in C minor, that stamped Brahms as the legitimate representative of the great dynasty of German composers. It had been long expected;

BRAHMS IN HIS LIBRARY

for the musical world must have realized that the man who could show himself so great a master of thematic development as Brahms had done in many chamber compositions (the last of which were the three string quartets, Opp. 51 and 67, and the quartet for piano and strings, Op. 60), and who could handle the orchestra so skilfully as he had handled it in the "Haydn" variations, could give the world a new symphonic masterpiece. As such the work in C minor could hardly be universally accepted at once; if it had not stirred up opposition and discussion, its real importance might well have been questioned, but by this time Brahms himself most probably cared but little for the opinions of friendly or adverse critics, although his warm heart was always appreciative of the enthusiasm of his intimate friends; and the verdict of such people as Joachim and Frau von Herzogenberg was always eagerly awaited by him. In many cases their criticisms were followed, and alterations made in deference to them. The first symphony is one of the great landmarks in the history of Brahms's popularity in England; for when it was quite new the University of Cambridge offered to the composer and to Joachim the honorary degree of Mus.D., which cannot be granted *in absentia.* Joachim would in any case be in England, and Brahms hesitated for some time whether to accept the invitation, but finally refused it in consequence of the publication of a premature announcement concerning his appearance at the Crystal Palace. He acknowledged the compliment of the University by allowing the first English performance of the new symphony to take place at a concert given by the Cambridge University Musical Society on 8 March, 1877, and it was conducted by Joachim, who contributed his own *Elegiac Overture*, conducting it himself, and playing the solo part of Beethoven's concerto.

The second symphony was not long in following upon the first, for it was given at the Vienna Philharmonic on 11 December, 1877, and at Leipzig in January, 1878; and the orchestral vein so successfully struck was further worked in the violin concerto which Joachim introduced to the Gewandhaus public and to the world on 1 January, 1879.[1]

Two important works for pianoforte solo belong to the same period, Opp. 76 and 79, as well as the first of the three sonatas for pianoforte and violin, Op. 78. The tender, winsome grace of the last must have won Brahms almost more friends than any of his previous compositions, and the impression was deepened by the production of the two overtures, Opp. 80 and 81, the *Academic Festival Overture* and the *Tragic Overture.*

In 1880, in the course of his duties as a member of a commission for the annual grant of Government stipends to young artists (on which he had served since 1875), he came across the early efforts of Anton Dvořák, and at once became a warm admirer of his music, in spite of so many points at which the artistic ideals of the two men diverged. In 1878 Brahms had undertaken the first of several Italian journeys in company with his great friend, Dr. Theodor Billroth. In 1881 began the pleasant associations with the court of Saxe-Meiningen, brought about by the enthusiasm of von Bülow, the conductor of the

[1] A doubt has lately been raised, and is to be found in the analytical programmes of many performances of the concerto, as to whether the first performance of the work took place at Leipzig or at Berlin. There is no question at all that it was given first at the Leipzig Gewandhaus on 1 January, 1879. Unfortunately, the English translator of Moser's *Joseph Joachim* has made a tiresome blunder, stating on p. 263 that Joachim performed it for the first time in public at one of the Hochschule concerts. Reference to the original (p. 240) shows at once that the words "in Berlin" have been left out by the translator, and that Moser makes no claim that Berlin heard the first actual performance.

Autograph letter from Brahms to a correspondent unknown (but not impossibly Sir George Grove), relating to the death of C. F. Pohl, the biographer of Haydn, who died in Vienna in April, 1887. Facsimile included by kind permission of the Brahms-Gesellschaft, and of W. Barclay Squire, Esq., the owner of the original letter.

TRANSLATION

"DEAR AND MUCH HONOURED SIR,—

"Please accept at this time my thanks and friendly greetings. Things have not altered with us much of late [literally, In our case the recently or quickly passed time has not signified much]. We still deplore our friend most sincerely. I am as grateful as I was before for your expressions of feeling. In the course of the winter I have seen our sick friend often, never without his remembering you affectionately. He never lacked sympathy and loving care, and the excellent people with whom he lived are highly to be commended in that respect. A few days before his death, I went to Italy, and only found your letter when I returned to Thun.

"It was a great pleasure to me to read your words, and to know them addressed to myself. Will you let me again thank you for them? My thanks come from the heart, as they must when I think of our friend, the best and most affectionate fellow on earth. With hearty greetings,

"Your devoted,

"J. BRAHMS"

Thun in der Schweiz.

Lieber u. sehr geehrter
Herr

Nehmen Sie, ich bitte,
auch heute noch meinen
Dank u. Gruß freundlichst.
In unserem Fall bedeutet
ja die längst verflossene
Zeit nicht viel. Wir
betrauern heute noch gleich
herzlich unseren Freund u. daß
es Sie drängte, mir Ihre
Empfindungen darüber

nachzusprechen, angefügt
ich hätte so dankbar wie damals.
Jenen Ludwig II. Wiedersehen
habe ich den kranken Freund
oft gesehen, auch einmal
ohne daß er auch noch Ihrer
in Liebe gedachte.
An Schonung u. Lebensalter
Pflege hat es ihm nicht ge-
fehlt, die unterschiedlichen Ärzte
aber, bei denen er weilte,
waren gänzlich unzulänglich.
Wenige Tage vor seinem
Tode sah ich auch Vater.

u. Freund Ihres Andenkens war
als ich s. Z. Ihre Zeilen auch
Ihren Brief.
Ich war auch eine ungemein
angenehme Ueberraschung
Ihre Worte zu lesen u. an
mich gerichtet zu wissen.
Wollen Sie meinen Dank
dafür auch heute noch gelten
lassen. Es kommt von Herzen,
wie das zu dem Andenken
des ersten Freundes, des gütigsten
u. liebevollsten Menschen auf
der Welt, nicht anders sein kann.

Mit herzlichem Gruß

Ihr

sehr ergebener

J. Brahms.

famous orchestra. The composer played his new pianoforte concerto with that body in 1882, and an odd result of the friendship with the Duke was the undertaking set on foot by Bülow of taking the Meiningen orchestra to Leipzig, to show how certain works of Brahms should be performed. The C minor symphony was in the programme, as well as the first pianoforte concerto, which Bülow played, the band accompanying without a conductor. The third symphony (Vienna Philharmonic, under Richter, 2 December, 1883) and the fourth (Meiningen, 25 October, 1885) put the crown on the master's orchestral achievements.

For about ten years Brahms had now enjoyed the reward of his lifelong work and happy labours. As in the early part of his career his works had been held to be obscure, unintelligible, and ugly, so now a new style of attack on his music was led by Hugo Wolf, when hard up and disappointed, and therefore the more easily to be forgiven, although his animadversions were bitterly resented at the time. In England we are not unfamiliar with the sort of invective which, consciously or unconsciously, has been based upon Wolf's diatribes. With the exception of such irritating experiences—and what great man was ever free from them for long?—the later years of the composer's life were very happy ones. Surrounded by intelligent and devoted friends who understood all his little idiosyncrasies and humoured him in every way, the routine of his life, with the regular journeys to Ischl or some such resort in the summer, and to Italy in the spring (until 1893), must have been tranquil and fruitful in musical suggestion.

For the record of the latest period of his career is really contained in a few casual reminiscences by his intimate friends, and above all in the beautiful works which glorified the last decade of his life. It is the decade of the pianoforte pieces, Opp. 116–19, of the German folk-songs, of the works suggested by the masterly clarinet playing of Professor Mühlfeld, and of those wonderful *Ernste Gesänge* which close the master's list of compositions with such noble meditations on death and what lies beyond the grave. These were partly inspired by the death of Frau Schumann on 20 May, 1896, which was a terrible shock to Brahms; mentally, he was grievously afflicted by it, and physically he never completely recovered from a chill caught at her funeral. Between this time and his own death the only work he accomplished was the arrangement of a set of eleven chorale-preludes for the organ, written at various dates, though not published till after his death.

In September, 1896, he went to Carlsbad for a cure; he suffered very greatly during the winter, but managed to attend several concerts, such as those given by the Joachim Quartet in Vienna in January (when his G major quintet was played with great success), the Philharmonic Concert of 7 March, when his fourth symphony and Dvořák's violoncello concerto (a piece for which he had unbounded admiration) were played, and he went twice to the opera. He passed away—the cause of death being degeneration of the liver—in the presence of his kind housekeeper, Frau Celestine Truxa, on 3 April, 1897, at the lodging, 4, Carlsgasse, where he had lived quietly for a quarter of a century. He was buried in the Central Friedhof on 6 April, and many were the memorial concerts given in his honour all the world over.

By a strange mischance, a will about which he consulted his old friends Dr. and Frau Fellinger was not executed, and the only valid testament was in the form of a letter to Simrock, the publisher. There were complications of various kinds, sundry cousins making claims to the master's property. Ultimately a compromise was arrived at, with the result that "the blood relations have been recognised as heirs to all but the library, which is now in the possession of the Gesellschaft der Musikfreunde; that Frau Truxa's legacy has been paid, and that certain sums accepted by the societies [the Liszt Pensionverein of Hamburg, the Czerny Verein, and the Gesellschaft der Musikfreunde], by which they will ultimately benefit, have been invested, and the income arising from them secured for the payment of the life-annuity to Herr Schnack"[1] [the son of Frau Caroline Brahms, who died in 1902].

The first monument to the master's memory was that executed by Hildebrandt, which was uncovered at Meiningen on 7 October, 1899. On the seventieth anniversary of the master's birth, 7 May, 1903, a monument, designed by Fräulein Ilse Conrat, was erected at the grave. Five years later, on the same anniversary, another monument was inaugurated at Vienna, the work of Rudolf Weyr; and on the "birthday" in 1909 a monument by Max Klinger was unveiled at Hamburg, near the entrance to the new Musikhalle, and a commemorative tablet was placed on the house where Brahms stayed at Düsseldorf. Houses in which he lived at Vienna, Ischl, and Thun have been decorated in the same way. A Brahms Museum, planned so as to conform exactly to the dimensions of Brahms's rooms at Ischl, and to contain the furniture from those rooms, has been founded at Gmünden by Dr. Victor von Miller zu Aichholz, who has collected many autographs and personal relics of all kinds.

It would be difficult to name any famous man who had so great an objection as Brahms had to the habit of wearing his heart upon his sleeve. He carried his

[1] Miss May's *Life*, ii. 290.

characteristic reticence so far that his brusquerie of manner is the feature most familiar to the readers of the books about him. There are already many hundreds of stories, some of them no doubt true, which show a certain mischievous disposition, especially towards people whom he suspected of a wish to "lionize" him; but his quiet acts of kindness more than counterbalance these superficial eccentricities, which after all seem more like the small transgressions of a vigorous child. There were numberless points in which he remained a child throughout his life, as though he trailed his clouds of glory longer than most men. That he should have been devoted to his tin soldiers as a child is of course nothing at all remarkable, but it is rather significant that he should have carefully kept them in his possession until he was twenty-eight years old, and have shown them to his friend Dietrich, saying that he could not bear to part with them.[1] He shared with many of the great men of the world a faculty for going to sleep at a moment's notice, and rising refreshed after only a few minutes' slumber. It is undoubtedly true that he was careless in the matter of dress, and that he hated anything like ceremonial customs or stiff behaviour; on the platform his manner of bowing (in 1859) was, according to Joachim, like the action of a swimmer who comes to the surface and shakes the water from his hair.[2] Official recognition of his eminence meant less than nothing to him; his indifference was by no means a pose, but was just the result of the hatred he felt towards certain sycophantic recipients of court favour. Much was formerly heard of his bluff ways, which no doubt did often cause pain to many sensitive souls; but the publication of his correspondence with such

[1] *Recollections*, by Dietrich and Widmann, trans., pp. 37, 38.
[2] Litzmann, *Clara Schumann*, iii. 48.

intimates as the Herzogenbergs, J. O. Grimm, Joachim, and, above all, Madame Schumann, shows how delicate was his tact in the real things of life, how ready he was to show his practical sympathy with other people, though his friends may have had to humour his little idiosyncrasies in the matter of his personal habits and comforts, and how truly generous was his nature. Once, when leaving his parents' home after a visit to them (when his own means had become comparatively ample for his needs), he put a number of bank-notes between the pages of his copy of Handel's *Saul*, and said to his father when taking leave, "Dear father, if things go badly with you, the best consolation is always in music. Read carefully in my old *Saul* and you'll find what you want." His loving care for Frau Schumann, for his stepmother and her son, and for others who looked to him for help of one kind or another, is abundantly clear, and a larger-minded or more open-handed man surely never lived. He appreciated the pleasures of life and was not afraid to let his enjoyment be seen; yet he was no voluptuary, careless of the ultimate destiny of the race or of the individual. Even if we had nothing to go by but the words of his choral works, we should know that the problems of human destiny, of life, death, and immortality, engrossed him throughout his life. The *Schicksalslied*, *Rhapsodie*, *Requiem*, the two motets, Op. 74, and the part-songs, Op. 104, tell us, even without the evidence of the *Serious Songs*, which were the last publication of his life, that he was an earnest thinker, and that he had faced the great questions bravely and had found an answer to them which for him was sufficient. While shrinking from the dogmas of the Churches, and very shy of owning the beliefs he held, he yet shows his deep conviction of the immortality of the soul and a sure and certain hope of its future happiness. In letters to Frau von Herzogenberg,[1] he asks her to find "heathenish" words from Scripture for him to set, meaning thereby such texts as appear in the first three of the *Serious Songs*. Though the landmarks of religions might be removed, though doctrines that guided the lives of his ancestors might be assailed and discredited, though the higher criticism might seem to demolish the credibility of the Scripture records, yet a great and merciful system is dimly apprehended, and upon this he relies for comfort and guidance. The publication of the commonplace-book in which he wrote favourite extracts from the literature of different countries[2] has thrown a fresh light on his own inner life, and illustrates his big, healthy nature (see p. 36).

This may be a convenient place to attempt a summary of the Brahms literature, including the Lives and the published correspondence, the issue of which makes the biographer's task especially easy in the present day.

The first authoritative life of the master, by Dr. Hermann Deiters, appeared in the *Sammlung musikalischer Vorträge* in 1880; it was translated into English by Rosa Newmarch, and published, with additions, in 1888; reissued after the master's death, in 1898.

J. B. Vogel's *Johannes Brahms, sein Lebensgang*, appeared in 1888.

Heinrich Reimann's *Johannes Brahms* was published, without date, by the Berlin *Harmonie*, as one of a useful series of illustrated monographs on great composers. It appeared soon after the composer's death, with a slip inserted at the beginning giving the date of that death as 1896!

[1] *Correspondence*, i. 200; trans., 274.

[2] *Des jungen Kreislers Schatzkästlein, herausgegeben von Johannes Brahms*, was published by the Brahms-Gesellschaft in 1908.

Max Kalbeck's exhaustive biography of the master, the most thoroughgoing work of its kind, is not yet completed, and it is doubtful whether the difficulties which arose after the second instalment was published will ever be surmounted. The first volume appeared in 1904, carrying the narrative of his life only as far as 1862; the second, completed in 1909 (in two half-volumes), goes down to 1874.

A remarkably good and complete biography was written by Miss Florence May, and published in two volumes in 1905. The author had previously contributed some "Personal Recollections of Brahms" to a short-lived periodical, *The Musical Gazette* (published by Joseph Williams in 1902).

H. C. Colles's *Brahms* (John Lane, 1908) contains a wonderful amount of valuable information in a small space.

Erinnerungen an Johannes Brahms, by Albert Dietrich and J. V. Widmann (1898), were issued in an English translation by Dora Hecht in 1899, and published by Seeley & Co.

The letters of the eminent surgeon Dr. Theodor Billroth, one of the most intimate friends of Brahms, himself an enthusiastic musician and writer on the art, contain many interesting details of the master.

Joachim's oration at the unveiling of the Meiningen monument in 1899 was published as *Zum Gedächtniss des Meisters Johannes Brahms*.

The *Neues Wiener Tageblatt* for 9 May, 1901, contains H. von Meysenbug's *Aus Johannes Brahms' Jugendtagen*, and the same periodical on 3 and 4 April in the following year printed K. von Meysenbug's contribution with the same title.

The *Jahrbuch* of the Gesellschaft Hamburgischer

Kunstfreunde for 1902 contains an interesting series of *Brahms-Erinnerungen aus dem Tagebuch von Frau Wasserbaudirector Lentz, geb. Meier.*

The account of the Vienna monument, *Zur Enthüllung des Brahms-Denkmal in Wien*, 7 *Mai*, 1908, contains some interesting articles. A picture of the monument itself is inserted facing page 34.

A special Brahms number of the periodical called *Die Musik*, issued May, 1903, contains various articles and illustrations. The Brahms-Gesellschaft, founded after the master's death, has done excellent work in publishing his correspondence, as well as in other ways. Six volumes have already appeared, containing the master's own letters and those of his correspondents. Vols. I. and II. contain the correspondence with Herr and Frau von Herzogenberg, edited by Max Kalbeck, 1908. They have been translated by Hannah Bryant, and published by John Murray, London, in 1909. The husband and wife were in some ways the most intimate friends of Brahms, with the exception of Joachim and Madame Schumann. Both the Herzogenbergs were accomplished musicians, the husband a composer of some distinction, the wife skilled in interpretation, and possessed of a remarkable insight and critical faculty. Both allowed themselves to criticize each new work of Brahms with perfect freedom, and it is interesting to see how often he took their hints and acted upon them. These volumes are especially interesting to students of the details in Brahms's workmanship, though very often the reader is struck by his disregard of some important question put to him by Frau von Herzogenberg, or by his habit of dismissing what she says with a curt word or two that falls oddly on English ears accustomed to the conventional courtesies of daily life. The impres-

BRAHMS' MONUMENT AT VIENNA

sion made by these two volumes is that the bulk of the actual material of the letters comes from the Herzogenbergs rather than from Brahms; but in the third volume of the series (edited by Wilhelm Altmann) Brahms is the chief writer. The letters deal with the composition and the first performance of the *Requiem*, and are of the highest value to students of that work. Reinthaler organized the quasi-complete performance of the *Requiem* in Bremen Cathedral on 10 April, 1868; and the correspondence about that work, as well as about later compositions of the master, is most interesting. The letters range from 1867 until Reinthaler's death in 1896. The next division of the book contains six letters of Brahms to Max Bruch, with nine from Bruch to Brahms, which deal principally with Bruch's works rather than with those of Brahms, although there are passages concerning the *Requiem* to be found in them. To Hermann Deiters Brahms wrote a good many details concerning his works, notably the "Haydn" variations and the two overtures; these are printed next with a single letter to Professor Heïmsoeth, of Bonn, about the Schumann festival of 1873. A few short communications from Brahms to Reinecke, of no great importance, lead to the correspondence with Professor Rudorff, a section of great interest, spread over the years 1865 to 1886. There are two facsimiles of the corrections undertaken by Brahms and Rudorff respectively of a corrupt passage in the score of a flute concerto of Mozart; and some details concerned with the edition of Chopin's complete works are given. The last section of the volume contains letters to and from Bernhard Scholz and his wife, who were among the closer friends of the composer; it will be remembered that Scholz was one of the four signatories of the famous protest. The correspondence dates from 1874 to 1882, or rather those dates cover all the letters that have been preserved. Julius Otto Grimm, the remaining signatory of the protest, whose correspondence with Brahms occupies the fourth volume of the series, edited by Richard Barth, was the master's friend from 1853, and outlived him by six years, although he was six years older. The volume gives us a representative picture of all the different sides of Brahms's nature, for there are plenty of boyish jokes enshrined in it, as well as discussions on music, and many references to the lady, Agathe von Siebold, upon whom Brahms's affections were fixed at the time of his tenure of the post at the court of Lippe-Detmold, and who lived at Göttingen, where Grimm was director of the Musical Academy. The fifth and sixth volumes of the letters, edited by Andreas Moser, take us into the inmost shrine of Brahms's life, for they contain the correspondence with Joachim, and show us the faithful picture of the wonderful friendship which produced such rich fruit in the history of music. With these, and the letters to and from Madame Schumann, published in the third volume of her Life by Litzmann (1908,) the reader is admitted into the close intimacy of the master.

The Brahms-Gesellschaft also printed the extract-book or commonplace-book in which Brahms put down passages that struck him in the literature of many countries. He called it *Des jungen Kreislers Schatzkästlein*—and this title is kept by the editor, Carl Krebs, who issued it in 1908 in a cover in imitation of the original paper-bound book. It contains over six hundred aphorisms and quotations from all manner of sources, as well as a number of weighty sentences by Joachim, marked " F. A. E." (see pp. 32, 49).

The English reader may be directed to some important

contributions to the Brahms literature, such as the following:—

Studies in Modern Music, by W. H. Hadow, second series, 1895.

Studies in Music, reprinted from *The Musician*, 1901, contains an article on Brahms by the late Philipp Spitta.

James Huneker's *Mezzotints in Modern Music* contains an article on Brahms, called "The Music of the Future."

Daniel Gregory Mason's *From Grieg to Brahms*, New York, 1905, has a thoughtful article.

J. L. Erb's *Brahms* is a summary published in Dent's *Master Musicians*, 1905.

The *Contemporary Review* for 1897 contains an article on "Brahms and the Classical Position."

Georg Henschel read a paper on "Personal Recollections" of the composer before the Royal Institution in 1905.

In French some very interesting books were written by the late Hugues Imbert, who did a great work in obtaining a hearing for Brahms in France. His chief book on the subject is *Johannes Brahms, sa vie et son œuvre*, Paris, 1906.

The later editions of the dictionaries of Grove and Riemann contain extensive articles.

CHAPTER II

BRAHMS AND HIS CONTEMPORARIES

AS a supplement to the necessarily meagre summary of the outward events in the life of Brahms, it may not be uninteresting to touch upon his own preferences in music, to trace the course by which his works became known throughout the world, to consider the influence of his contemporaries upon him, and to gather as far as may be possible the opinions formed about him by musicians of different generations. The first is, of course, far less important than the rest, for composers are most rarely dowered with the critical faculty, and the only value we can set upon the opinions even of a Brahms is for the sake of the light they throw upon his own nature. The fact, for example, that *Carmen* was one of the composer's favourite operas does not affect our estimate of that work one way or another. It is unlikely that any of the Brahms enthusiasts think more highly of it because he admired it, and we may do his professed detractors the justice to suppose that none of them has gone so far as to slight Bizet's masterpiece because Brahms praised it. But it is of no little interest to the student of his character to know that he could heartily admire the frank, straightforward melodies and the characterization of a work so very far removed in style from what are generally supposed to be the distinguishing marks of his own music. It is of far greater importance to make clear the attitude of Brahms towards the work of Wagner, an attitude concerning which so many misstatements have been industriously circulated, that too much stress can hardly be laid upon the actual facts of the case. In German musical circles there has for many years been a habit of making sharp divisions between the admirers of any two great contemporaries. The harm it did in the case of Mendelssohn and Schumann is well known to every student of musical history; and while the musical world of Germany continues to find a great part of its artistic enjoyment in the diversion of splitting itself into opposing camps, no observer can wonder that Brahms should have been set up, entirely against his will, as the chief bulwark against the music of the new school. About the year 1860 the materials for a new arrangement of parties were just preparing, and the main difficulty in the way of a comfortable split was the personality and the art of Schumann himself. He had founded the *Neue Zeitschrift*, and in many ways had shown himself in the advanced ranks of his time, so that the "new" party could by no means dispense with his name; on the other hand, he had declared himself, with what might be almost called his last words to the world, a champion of the music of Brahms, who, a few years before, had definitely severed himself from the "new" party. These latter, having celebrated the 25th anniversary of the foundation of Schumann's periodical by a festival of four days in 1859, arranged a festival in Schumann's special honour, at his birthplace, Zwickau, in June, 1860. A general invitation was issued to all music-lovers to attend the festival; but beyond this, neither Madame Schumann, Joachim, nor Brahms received any further communication with regard to the celebration. It may not have been intentionally done in order to slight those who stood nearest to Schumann in life, but the net result to the "new" party was that the marked absence of these intimates on such an occasion could be conveniently turned to the uses of the combatants, as it was of course implied that they had stayed away out of jealousy.

From this time forth, the "new" school was never tired of trying to make out that Schumann's friends wanted to keep his music and his fame as a kind of private property of their own, and even that the true traditions of Schumann's music were not to be found among those who knew him best. This assumption of the Liszt party may even now be occasionally observed in criticism, but of course there was not the slightest foundation for supposing that the "classical" party ever thought of making themselves into a kind of sect. They were ultimately forced into completely breaking with the "new" party, but it was the new party with which lay the responsibility for the cleavage. With regard to Liszt's most representative works, the symphonic poems, Brahms shared with Wagner and Joachim the unfavourable opinions which Wagner could not very well express, as the others were perfectly free to do; but for the art of Wagner himself Brahms had nothing but admiration. In the correspondence with Joachim at the time of the unfortunate protest against the Weimar fabrications, Brahms is careful to make it clear that he does not include Wagner among the men whose influence he wishes to counteract.[1] What has been called the "Wahnfried" atmosphere, with its hothouse exhalations, could never have been congenial to Brahms, and the personalities of

[1] See *Joachim Correspondence*, i. 274.

the two composers may very well have been rather antagonistic, even if Wagner and his friends and satellites had refrained from attacking him. It is perhaps necessary to recall the manners and customs of the early Wagnerians in order that we may realize how much that was repulsive would have had to be endured by a clean-minded, earnest and catholic musician who should join their ranks. None of the professed Wagnerians knew, and very few loved, the music-dramas better than Brahms did, and it is on record that he very rarely missed a performance of Wagner's later works in Vienna.[1]

An interesting account is given by Kalbeck[2] of the single interview between Brahms and Wagner at Penzing, near Vienna, in 1863, when the former, lately come to Vienna, played his "Handel" variations in a manner which called forth unstinted praise of the work and the performance from the older master. The unfortunate episode concerning the autograph of Wagner's "new Venusberg music" from *Tannhäuser* could not but spoil the relations between the two composers (it had been committed by Wagner to the charge of Peter Cornelius, and he, imagining it had been a gift, gave it to Brahms, who valued it highly; the letters which passed between the composers on the occasion were of a kind it is difficult to forget); but even if the misunderstanding had not occurred, the natures of the two men were too unlike to have allowed any real intercourse between them. We cannot picture Brahms arraying himself in gorgeous stuffs when he wished to compose, or surrounding himself with a court of flatterers who should keep from him the least

[1] See the *Herzogenberg Correspondence*, i. 183 (trans., 159), and note. Also Litzmann's *Clara Schumann*, iii. 236.

[2] *Life*, ii. 114-17.

breath of adverse criticism. But, apart from constitutional diversity, Brahms understood and sympathized with Wagner's music at a time when the Wagner cause was still to be won.

The exact opposite of this is true in regard to the relations of Brahms with Tchaikovsky. The account of their meeting at Hamburg in 1889 shows that "the personality of Brahms, his purity and loftiness of aim, and earnestness of purpose, won Tchaikovsky's sympathy. Wagner's personality and views were, on the contrary, antipathetic to him; but his music awoke his enthusiasm, while the works of Brahms left him unmoved to the end of his life."[1] It is well known that the art of each of the two had little which could appeal to the other. It may be suggested that there was a reason for this quite apart from the polemics which have so much to do with music on the Continent. Brahms, as we shall see, had a special liking for themes built on the successive notes of a chord; it is one of Tchaikovsky's most obvious characteristics that in his most beautiful and individual subjects, the movement is what is called "conjunct"; that is, the successive notes are those of a scale, not of a chord. Almost every theme in the "Pathetic" symphony, to take the best-known instance, is formed in this way, and a careful study of the Russian's themes from this point of view of structure will show a surprising preponderance of those which are built on successive notes of the scale. The difference is perhaps not one that would be obvious at once, least of all to the composers themselves, for it is probable that neither was conscious of his own predilections in the formation of themes; but for this very reason complete sympathy would be the less easy to establish

[1] *Grove's Dictionary* (2nd ed.), v. 39.

between them. Remembering, too, that one was pre-eminently a colourist, the other pre-eminently a draughtsman, the wonder would have been if they had appreciated one another's music. The same cause might, it is true, be supposed to interfere with Brahms's admiration of Wagner, since Wagner was the greatest pioneer of orchestral colouring in modern music; but the works of the great music-dramatist stand so obviously apart from the rest of music, and in particular from the classical models, that they could be thoroughly enjoyed as complete art-products in their own way, even by a champion of the classical tradition.

The figure of Rubinstein loomed large on the world in his lifetime, and it is of some interest to see what he and Brahms thought of each other. Kalbeck[1] gives an extract from a letter of Rubinstein's to Liszt, in which the virtuoso's first impressions are amusingly summed up:—

"Pour ce qui est de Brahms, je ne saurais pas trop préciser l'impression qu'il m'a faite; pour le salon, il n'est pas assez gracieux, pour la salle de concert, il n'est pas assez fougueux, pour les champs, il n'est pas assez primitif, pour la ville, pas assez général—j'ai peu de foi en ces natures-là." Another less agreeable reference to Brahms is reported at secondhand in Bülow's letters, and we may hope that Rubinstein never made it: "Si j'avais voulu courtiser la presse, on n'entendrait pas parler ni de Wagner ni de Brahms." It is hardly necessary to point out that of all men who ever lived, Brahms was the least likely to *courtiser la presse*, while Rubinstein lost no opportunity of adding to the very temporary edifice of his renown as a composer. Unfortunately, we have no

[1] i. 268.

record of what Brahms's opinion was of Rubinstein's music, beyond a passing reference to his ways of composing, and in particular, to a sight Brahms once had of a set of perfectly blank music-pages provided with a full title and opus-number, before a note of the songs had been written.[1] Rubinstein's appreciation of the music of Brahms seems to have been limited to a performance of a movement from the D major serenade at one of the concerts of the Music Society of St. Petersburg in 1864. At his later historical pianoforte recitals not a note of Brahms was played, although he conducted choral works of his on various occasions.

Although there is no record of Brahms being present at the performance of Verdi's operas in his Italian journeys, his admiration for the Italian master's *Requiem* was hearty, immediate, and sincere. One of Hans von Bülow's not infrequent alterations of opinion was in regard to this composition, against which he spoke at first with characteristic lack of moderation. Some time after Brahms had expressed his delight in it, Bülow changed his mind, as he did with fine generosity in respect to the music of Brahms himself. German writers have spent much time in debating why Brahms wrote no opera, and one of them, Alfred Kühn by name, went so far as to invent an interview with the composer on the subject. The upshot of the story, quoted from the *Strassburger Post* of 13 April, 1897, may be read in J. K. Widmann's *Recollections*,[2] and it is clear that the master was in no way disinclined to write an opera if a good libretto was forthcoming. He discussed many subjects with Widmann, but, as all the world knows, the cantata *Rinaldo* remains the only example of how he might have treated opera had

[1] Kalbeck, ii. 179, note 2.

[2] English trans., 107.

he found a good book. Looking at his completed work as a whole, it is easy to see that his subtle way of dealing with deep emotions, which comes out in so many of the songs, must have been lost on the stage or abandoned for a more superficial style which would not have been truly congenial or characteristic. It is curious to learn from the same source [1] that Brahms considered the ideal conditions of opera to consist in a combination of spoken dialogue or *recitativo secco*, with set-pieces for the lyrical climaxes. It would have been difficult even for Brahms to obtain the approval of the world at large for a method of operatic writing which must be considered a little reactionary in the present day; and while the method of continuous music had the weighty support of Wagner and all the typically modern composers of all nations, it would have been a miracle if an opera composed on the other system, even by a great master, had really succeeded. On the whole we need not regret that Brahms left the operatic stage to others. The kindly interest he took in the career of Hermann Goetz was no doubt largely due to compassion for his state of health; he greatly admired *The Taming of the Shrew*, but regretted the posthumous production of *Francesca da Rimini*, though he had aided with his counsel those who undertook to complete the work; but the two men were so widely different in character and disposition that they never could have become intimate, even if Brahms had not unintentionally wounded Goetz's supersensitive nature by asking him, "Do you also amuse yourself with such things?" when he saw some newly written sheets of music on his desk. Of course Goetz was wrong to be annoyed, and his solemn reply, "That is the holiest thing I possess!" naturally piqued Brahms, who

[1] *Recollections*, English trans., 108, 109, 112.

always resented any self-importance on the part of musicians, and to whom any hint of pomposity was all his life most obnoxious. The offhand manner of hiding deep feelings under a jest is a kind of shyness more common with Englishmen than with Germans, but we cannot quite excuse Brahms for the many occasions on which his manner gave offence to harmless people.

The stories concerning this peculiarity of his are very numerous, and there are many more which can be ascribed to nothing but sheer love of mischief. Once, at Baden-Baden, while he was taking his ease under a tree in his garden, a stranger advanced towards him and delivered a little complimentary speech, evidently prepared beforehand, of course expressing boundless admiration for Brahms's music. The stock-in-trade of the interviewer was a little too plainly displayed, and Brahms yielded to his love of mischief, and stopped the speech with the words, "Stop, my dear sir, there must be some mistake here. I have no doubt you are looking for my brother, the composer; I'm sorry to say he has just gone out for a walk, but if you make haste and run along that path, through the wood, and up another hill, you may possibly still catch him up." On another occasion a young girl-pianist was allowed to turn over the pages of a new composition for the piano which Madame Schumann was to read through for the first time from Brahms's autograph. The composer took the girl aside and explained to her that at one point two leaves were to be turned over at once, the portion between them being omitted, and that at another the leaf was to be turned before the bottom of the page was reached; various other directions were given, to which the young lady paid, as was natural, the most careful attention. Her obedience to the master's orders led to awful confusion, as the alteration did not really exist; she was reduced to tears, Madame Schumann was of course very angry with her, and we can only hope that Brahms took the blame of the not very pretty joke upon himself. His boyishness of disposition is noticed by many of his contemporaries, and it was by no means always mischievous. Many were the graceful things he said in congenial company, even when the hated "lionizing" process seemed to be within sight. The landlord of a certain restaurant at Vienna was asked to produce his best wine for some friends whom Brahms took to dine there, and remarked, "Here is a wine that surpasses all others, as much as the music of Brahms does that of other composers." "Well, then," says Brahms, "take it away, and bring us a bottle of Bach!"

In travelling in Italy, or other Catholic countries, he showed a degree of tact that is rare among Englishmen, and almost unknown among Germans, by taking holy water on entering a church, and signing himself, in order not to scandalize any worshippers who might observe him. As a rule he was seen at his best in the company of Madame Schumann or of Joachim, both of whom stood in the closest relations to his artist soul. Nothing can be more charming than the letter in which he pressed Madame Schumann to visit him at Hamburg in 1861,[1] or more delicate than the way in which he tried to persuade her to accept a sum of money at a time when her funds were low and his above his needs. Still he was very apt to tease the poor lady, who never failed to be vexed at what was only meant in fun. Many instances from her point of view, showing how she felt his behaviour, occur in the third volume of her *Life*. In the

[1] Litzmann, *Clara Schumann*, iii. 109, 110.

Herzogenberg Correspondence[1] are some very amusing references to the needless terrors felt by Frau von Herzogenberg at the prospect of the *Feuerzauber* being played at a concert where Madame Schumann was to appear; Brahms's good sense carried off the affair quite successfully, and, as a matter of fact, Madame Schumann had the perseverance to go to two performances of *Die Walküre* a few years afterwards. A difference of opinion arose between Madame Schumann and Brahms, partly from a misunderstanding in regard to the complete edition of Schumann's works undertaken by his widow, and from the letters in Litzmann's life it is clear that she suffered much from the temporary coolness, which before long yielded to the old familiarity and affection.[2] No influence on Brahms was more salutary than that of the Schumanns, although it may be that he would have become more genial in mixed company, less uncertain in manner, if he had been intimate with men and women who lived more in the world than the Schumanns did. They and their circle would have thought it deceitful to assume a graciousness of demeanour they did not feel, and there are many instances in the lives of both of them which show that the amenities of ordinary social intercourse were rather neglected by them and their friends. Joachim may have learnt some of his wonderful unself-consciousness and simple courtesy by his intercourse with the world outside music; but beyond this there was in him an inherent instinct of thoughtfulness for the feelings of others, and a power of ordinary human sympathy which Brahms could, perhaps, hardly have acquired. The friendship between these two men is one of the most beautiful

[1] i. 44–9; trans., 38, etc.

[2] Litzmann, *Clara Schumann*, iii. 558 ff.

BRAHMS AND JOACHIM

things in musical history. It lasted, with one sad break,[1] down to the end of Brahms's life. For some years he and Joachim were in the habit of exchanging compositions and sketches for each other's criticism. The correspondence between the two shows that they stood on terms of absolute equality; throughout it is clear that Brahms had an enormously high opinion of Joachim's compositions,[2] and we need hardly refer to the loyalty with which the illustrious violinist made himself the champion of the music of Brahms. If, during the years of this profitable mutual criticism, either of the friends omitted to provide a composition at any of their meetings, a fine of a thaler was imposed, which the other spent in books for himself. The compositions exchanged were for the most part in contrapuntal style, and some of the canons, Op. 113, the chorale-prelude and fugue, and the *Geistliches Lied* for choir and organ, Op. 30, remain as the only surviving examples of the industry of Brahms, who wrote a great pile of music which he destroyed in later years. Of Joachim's influence on the music of Brahms there are many traces, even before the date of the A minor string quartet, Op. 51 No. 2, which begins with an allusion to the cryptic letters "F. A. E.," often used by the friends in their voluntary studies. They were taken as a motto by Joachim, and are understood to stand for "Frei, aber einsam" (Free, but alone). Every note that Brahms wrote for the violin, whether in chamber or orchestral music, was such as it would have been congenial to Joachim to play; and in the violin concerto, Op. 77, and the concerto for violin and violoncello, Op. 102, the special polyphonic effects in which Joachim was unrivalled among the

[1] See Kalbeck's *Life*, ii. 428–9, etc.

[2] *Joachim Correspondence*, i. 85.

violinists of all time, are found in abundance. As regards the world in general, it was Joachim, more than any one else, who started Brahms on his career by means of the memorable introduction to Schumann. It has been hinted before that Schumann's warm heralding of the new great master was not an unmixed benefit to him, as it necessarily prejudiced the German public against a man whose music was not yet generally accessible, and started the polemics which made so much noise in German musical circles. The temporary fiasco of the pianoforte concerto in 1859 naturally prejudiced a large section of the public against Schumann's protégé, and the appearance of Brahms's name as the first of only four signatures to the protest against the *Neue Zeitschrift für Musik*, in 1860, completed the split between the old school and the new.

It is quite clear that Brahms appreciated Liszt's playing, and even his character, although he could not quite swallow the symphonic poems; but of course with the Weimar school it must be all or nothing, and they ruled that no notice was henceforth to be taken of Brahms or his music. Even in the other camp it was long before his position was assessed at anything like its true greatness. Nothing in this need surprise us, although of course it is common for those who know the completed work of a man to reproach with blindness those to whom only his earliest efforts were accessible. A most interesting set of articles by Richard Pohl, in the *Neue Zeitschrift für Musik* for 1855,[1] shows the hesitation felt by the writer, who was anxious to see from Schumann's point of view, yet who felt unable fully to endorse his opinion. A quotation from them is to be found in Miss

[1] Pohl was an ardent champion of Wagner's music, who wrote over the signature "Hoplit."

May's *Life*.[1] An attitude common at that time is adopted by Bülow in a letter to Liszt, in which he refers to "Joachim and the statue of which he makes himself the pedestal." It is not unusual to see, in such antagonistic opinions of products that are afterwards universally acclaimed, the influence of prejudice or jealousy; but Miss May and Herr Kalbeck are careful to point out how sincere, for the most part, the adverse critics were. It is obviously impossible for the most enlightened and broad-minded critic to appreciate at once a new creation in art. His idioms must be accepted, his vocabulary must become more or less familiar, before we can possibly reach the clear thought that underlies them. In music, probably more than in any other art, that which is immediately accepted is for that very reason open to suspicion, for some of its component parts are probably of no great freshness, and will in the course of time be condemned as commonplace by the very men who hailed them most eagerly on a first acquaintance. It is the divine prerogative in great art of all kinds that it is not immediately received by all; but, while the great public is making a *furore* about something that is essentially commonplace, the more earnest and skilful critics are faced with the difficulty of discriminating between the rival merits of two things which at first may seem equally obscure. For there is naturally an obscurity which proceeds from lack of skill or inspiration, just as certainly as there is an obscurity caused by thought so weighty and original that it cannot be expressed in language of infantile simplicity. All that can be hoped for on behalf of a great new work of art is an attitude like that of the famous critic of Beethoven's C minor symphony: "I felt

[1] i. 189.

there was a door that was closed to me, but that behind the door mighty things were happening."

How gradually and surely the tide of public opinion went on flowing in Germany may be guessed from the various small attempts made by amateurs and professional musicians alike to set up some other composer as on a level with Brahms. To us, in the present day, it is hardly conceivable that a man like Raff can ever have been seriously considered as comparable to him in any way; yet at one time that prolific writer was spoken of as Brahms's rival, and at another Rubinstein's compositions were considered by a section of the public as having equal merits with his. There were persons in London, during the few years when Goetz's music was most in vogue in England, who were accustomed to point to the two composers' settings of Schiller's *Nänie*, and to express the opinion that Goetz's setting was so much the better of the two, that if he had only reached the natural term of human life he would have surpassed Brahms.

For some time such important centres as Leipzig and Vienna made it a point of honour to contradict each other's verdicts on the new compositions as they appeared, one receiving with special favour what the other had most distinctly condemned. As we saw in the summary of the master's biography, the period of the *Requiem* was the time when his greatness was first generally realized, and after that the game of pitting this or that writer against him seems to have lost some of its charm. There was a moment, indeed, when Max Bruch was considered a formidable rival, but by the time that Bülow uttered his famous toast to "the three B's of music," things had so far attained their true perspective that Bruch was probably the only person offended at the omission of his own name. Bruckner, the projector of colossal symphonies, was another who was more recently set up in competition with Brahms; but the occasional performances of his works in London are quite enough to check any desire to exalt him to an equal place in the musical hierarchy.

To Bülow belongs the credit of first performing a piece by Brahms in public; he played the first allegro of the C major sonata in Hamburg on 1 March, 1854. The distinction of giving the first public performance of one of his concerted works belongs to America, for William Mason introduced the trio in B, Op. 8, in New York on 27 November, 1855, nearly a month before its first performance in Germany, at Breslau. It was not till twelve years later that the propaganda of his music began in England with a performance of the first (B flat) sextet on 25 February, 1867,[1] at a Popular Concert, Mr. Chappell, the director of the institution, taking good care to protect himself from the stigma of bringing forward anything so revolutionary, by mentioning in a note in the programme that it was produced by request of Joachim. "No immediate result was perceptible from the performance," says Miss May, but there must have been many even then present who at least resolved to miss no future opportunity of hearing music from the same quarter, and we cannot doubt that the four following years saw a good deal of private interest in the composer, which was of course stimulated by Joachim, Madame Schumann, and Julius Stockhausen. The last-named artist conducted the memorable first English performance of the *Requiem* on 7 July, 1871, at the house of Sir Henry Thompson, when Lady Thompson and Cipriani Potter played the accom-

[1] It was repeated twice in 1873 with great success. See *Joachim Correspondence*, ii. 76.

paniments in a four-hand arrangement, and the solos were sung by Fräulein Anna Regan and Stockhausen. By that time a couple of duets from Op. 28 had been sung (also in private) by Madame Viardot-Garcia and Stockhausen, and the quartet in A for piano and strings had been produced at one of Ella's Musical Union Concerts at St. James's Hall. The students of the Royal Academy of Music, fired, no doubt, by the veteran Cipriani Potter, seem to have given a performance of the *Requiem* under Hullah, before its production by the Philharmonic Society on 2 April, 1873, under Cusins.[1] On this occasion Miss Sophie Ferrari and Santley were the soloists, and the former gave the soprano solo with her characteristic purity of style at the performance of the work by the Cambridge University Musical Society, under Sir C. Villiers Stanford, in 1876. An interesting list is given in Miss May's book[2] of first performances of various works by Brahms in England. In 1872 the D minor concerto was played at the Crystal Palace (solo, Miss Baglehole), and the G major sextet at St. George's Hall; in 1873 the Popular Concerts admitted two of the early Ballades, Op. 10, played by Madame Schumann, and Miss May introduced the "Handel" variations at the Crystal Palace. The latter pianist also brought forward the "Hungarian" variations from Op. 21 at the same place in 1874, and, if I am not mistaken, she has forgotten to mention her own playing of the "Paganini" variations for the first time in England, in their entirety, at a later date. The G minor quartet was played (possibly not for the first time in England) at the Popular Concerts (Madame Neruda playing the first violin) in 1874, and the quintet in F minor was played at the same concerts (with Joachim as

[1] See Miss May's *Life*, ii. 87, note.

[2] ii. 102, 103.

first violin) on 27 February, 1875. The year 1874 brought a performance of the *Serenade in A* for small orchestra at the Philharmonic Society under Cusins, and the two sets of *Liebeslieder Walzer* were heard for the first time in England in 1877, the earlier set, Op. 52, at the "Pops" in January, and the latter, Op. 65, at Cambridge in May. These last surprised the amateurs considerably, particularly those who had been under the impression that Brahms's music was always severe, "intellectual," and obscure. Both sets obtained immediate popularity, of which indeed they are always sure whenever six competent artists can be found who can preserve the proper balance between the predominant piano part and the subordinate vocal parts. From the seventies until the present day the popularity of the music of Brahms has continually increased in England, and in one department of executive music after another it has won its way. There are some who, from their memorable first experience of Brahms's music, have accepted its message, reverenced its creator, and awaited each new composition with the eager certainty that, even if it contained nothing appreciable by them at the first moment, there must be beauty and meaning which would become ultimately clear and well-beloved. These look back with amusement to the days when they were considered eccentric by their musical friends; and in all kinds of music it is remarkable to watch the difference in the public attitude towards Brahms. At a party given at Bremen in honour of the first performance of the *Requiem* in 1868, John Farmer, one of the earliest of the English Brahms enthusiasts, gave it as his opinion that if the performance had taken place in London people would have asked, "Is the fellow crazy?"[1]

[1] Miss May, ii. 75.

In the present day the vast spaces of St. Paul's Cathedral are crowded for the annual performance of the same work, which has even penetrated into the ken of the Royal Choral Society. The chamber music, as it was introduced at the Popular Concerts, was analysed in the programme-books in a way that was likely to check any enthusiasm the works might have excited; in the present day not only is it a prominent part of the repertory of chamber concerts and a constant delight to amateur performers, but even among the poorest of the working classes of London it has made itself friends, entirely without extraneous influence, explanatory commentaries, or anything of that kind. At one of the concerts given in the Northern Polytechnic, Holloway, by the People's Concert Society, after a quartet of Beethoven had been played, a working man was heard to remark, as he left the hall, "Ah, that's all very well, but give me my Brahms!" We may smile at his preference, but there is no doubting its genuineness. A sidelight is thrown on the present estimate of Brahms, as compared with the place he occupied twenty years ago, by a circumstance which any one will endorse who has written on music for the Press during that time. In the eighties and nineties it was an exceptional thing to find his name correctly spelt in proofs; it usually came out as "Braham," the tradition of that famous singer having lasted on through the years in the printers' world. Nowadays those who may wish to refer to the singer are generally obliged to restore the proper spelling of his name, the printers being apt to give it as "Brahms." A few years ago, soon after the composer's death, a rumour was spread (in consequence of this similarity of names) that he had actually visited England, a circumstance that had escaped all his biographers up to that time. When it was investigated an old man was discovered who declared that he well remembered seeing Brahms, and hearing him sing "The Death of Nelson"!

There are many of us who remember the usual verdict of the pianists of the late nineteenth century on the earlier piano solos of Brahms: "They may be very fine, but they are not piano music." Nowadays scarcely a recital programme is to be found which does not contain one of them, and the player's choice is by no means confined to the latest compositions for the instrument, in which we may admit that the peculiarities of *timbre* are more fully understood than in the earlier. Formerly even at a time when the *Liebeslieder* were received with delight, there were very few among the professional singers of London who ever ventured to perform one of the songs, unless it were the *Wiegenlied*, *Sonntag*, or *Die Mainacht;* nowadays we are no longer assured that Brahms wrote ineffectively for the voice, but he has been on all hands tacitly included among the great song-writers of the world, the peer of Schubert and Schumann. Last of all, his orchestral works, with or without solo instruments, have come into a larger share of popular favour. For many years Joachim was left in undisputed possession of the violin concerto, as the very few players who were musicians enough to appreciate it were naturally so much alarmed at the difficulties of the last movement that they found it convenient to join in the cry that the solo instrument was made too subordinate to the orchestra. It is a circumstance not altogether without its humorous side that every violinist of position in the present day, whatever his school, thinks it necessary to have this concerto in his repertory, and even quite immature performers, whose technique far exceeds their musicianship, venture to interpret it as well as they can in public.

At the earlier Richter concerts all the four symphonies were brought out and admirably given, and the interesting set of concerts at which Herr Steinbach conducted the Meiningen Orchestra drew much of their attraction from the performance of the series in chronological order. It was very long before the Queen's Hall authorities had enough faith in them to put them definitely into the repertory; but at last they got so far as to be included in the prospectus of the Promenade Concerts for 1908 (though they did not all reach the honour of actual performance); and lovers of the master may be quite certain that opportunities will abundantly increase for improving their acquaintance with his most individual works. For it must be remembered that in all great music, as in other products of art, there is an enormous driving power inherent in the product itself, which in the long run far exceeds that of the different opposing forces arrayed against it. Its admirers may be comparatively few in any given generation—they *must* be few at first—but whether they promulgate their opinions actively or not, their influence must be far greater, because exerted in one direction, than that of the antagonists whose objections to the work of art are in all probability based on various, it may be contradictory, prejudices. With all their apparatus for driving some worthless song into the ears of the public, by constant repetition at concerts organized for the purpose, the English publishers have not obtained more than a very short life for the most popular of the effusions they issue; but the influence of a noble song, like some masterpiece of Schubert, will go on spreading far and wide while the world lasts. Naturally the average publisher, treating the thing as a purely commercial speculation, knows his own business and makes his money over a popular success; but it is at least possible that, even in England alone, as many copies have been sold of the *Erlkönig* as of *Nancy Lee* (even though poor Schubert was glad enough to part with some of his finest songs for 10d. each), and from the large point of view the former is a more important achievement than the latter. It might be held that any very violent fit of exaggerated enthusiasm such as those from which the British public so often suffers, is of itself a mark of artistic shortcomings in the thing thus feverishly admired; attacks of this kind are inevitably followed by periods of reaction during which the real merits of the work of art are as much underestimated as they were before exaggerated. It is unnecessary to point to anything later than the music of Mendelssohn for an instance; there are already signs that after a long period of inflated popularity, and a shorter period of possibly unjust neglect by the leaders of musical fashion, it is slowly coming into a phase of recognition that may bear some relation to its real and ultimate value. It is perhaps not without significance that such a period of sudden, unreasoning popularity has never, even in England, been passed through by the music of Brahms. At no point since it began to be known has it been possible to say with truth, "The work of Brahms was formerly more popular than it is now." Year by year the growth in public estimation, if gradual, has been regular and widespread.

Those who began with liking a few of what they called his "more comprehensible" works will be familiar with the experience of finding that the obscurities of the others have disappeared, as it were, of themselves, while new worlds of beauty lie open to their investigation. Apart from Wagner in modern times—and his is hardly a parallel case, since there is so much that lies apart from music in the art which he himself perfected—it is difficult to find any composer but Brahms in the history of music of whom it could be said that at no time has his work been so highly appreciated as at present, until we come to the very greatest of all. For assuredly it is true of Bach and Beethoven, as it is of Brahms, that a love of their music has spread steadily through the civilized world from the moment when it first became accessible as a whole. None of the three, of course, lacked adverse criticism, and we know that each of them was galled by carping contemporaries. It is interesting and instructive to compare the famous obituary notice of Beethoven which adorns the ninth volume of the *Musical Quarterly Review* with various articles that appeared after the death of Brahms. A startling parallel is afforded in the non-committal tone of both, which the later writers would perhaps have hardly cared to suggest if they had realized how their words were contributing incidentally to place Brahms in the highest circle of the musical hierarchy.

It is fitting that some mention should be made of the various distinguished musicians who rank as the pioneers of the music of Brahms, those who bore the brunt of the attacks which were of course made upon it, and who so richly merit all the honour which Brahms's later admirers can give them. First and most important of all is Joseph Joachim, who gave Brahms the first helping hand in the introduction to Schumann, and who took the deepest interest in every one of his works as they came, identifying himself with Brahms's success in every possible way. The story of the intercourse of these two great men has already been told briefly, and the recently published correspondence between them throws new light on both men and their artistic relations. How through evil and good report Joachim championed the cause of his friend's music will be seen again when we come to consider the various works. Never had man a truer friend, and the oration spoken by Joachim at the unveiling of the Meiningen monument in 1899, from which quotation has already been made,[1] is among the noblest tributes ever paid by one man to another. Madame Schumann's name must rank with Joachim's among the earliest pioneers of the music of Brahms; her playing of the first piano concerto, and many of his masterpieces of chamber music, can never be forgotten by those who heard it; and though in England she naturally came before the public less often in his music than in that of her husband, it is worthy of record that at a London recital she won an encore for a "Sarabande" and "Gavotte" (whatever these may have been). Among other distinguished pianists who identified themselves with the master's music in the earlier days were Ignaz Brüll, whose performance of the F sharp minor sonata was famous; Fräulein Marie Baumeyer, the first lady to essay the B flat concerto in public; Charles Hallé, who played the same work for the first time in England, at Manchester; Miss Florence May, who introduced many of the most difficult pianoforte works at various concerts in London. Later on, Fräulein Ilona Eibenschütz, whose playing of the C major intermezzo from Op. 119 was really memorable; Mr. Borwick, identified with many of the later works, from the B flat concerto onwards; Miss Fanny Davies, whose enterprise gave us in England the first opportunity of becoming acquainted with the sonatas for clarinet and piano. Later artists have so

[1] See also *Herzogenberg Correspondence*, i. 161; trans., 140.

fully entered into the labours of these older interpreters that they can hardly rank as pioneers in any sense. Returning to the earliest of those who encouraged the composer by giving special performances, we must mention the American, William Mason (see p. 53).

Of the conductors who were associated with early performances the first to be mentioned is Julius Otto Grimm, who conducted many orchestral works at Göttingen; next come Reinthaler, who organized the first performance of the *Requiem* (six numbers only) in Bremen Cathedral in 1868; Reinecke, who directed the complete work in Leipzig in 1869; Richter, who gave many orchestral works in England for the first time. In later days, Von Bülow, whose conversion to the cause of Brahms has been already related; Fritz Steinbach, who, as director of the Meiningen Orchestra, was brought into close relations with the composer and received from him many authoritative readings. At Meiningen, too, began that friendship with Richard Mühlfeld, the eminent clarinettist, which had such weighty results during the composer's latest years of activity. Professor Hausmann, the famous violoncellist, for whom the double concerto was written, and the Rosé Quartet of Vienna, who gave the first performances of several pieces of the late chamber music, deserve special honour.

Of the singers who interpreted Brahms most successfully in the early days, Stockhausen was perhaps the most eminent, and his name was for long identified with the *Magelone-Lieder* and many other things; Madame Pauline Viardot-Garcia, who sang the alto part in the *Rhapsodie* for the first time; Frau Amalie Joachim, for whom were written the two songs with viola obbligato; Mademoiselle Antonie Kufferath (now Mrs. Edward Speyer), who san the seven songs, Op. 95, for the first time at Cologne in 1885; Fräulein Hermine Spies, whose singing of *Vergebliches Ständchen* will not soon be forgotten; Gustav Walter, the soloist in the first performance of *Rinaldo;* and particularly, as far as England is concerned, the party who first sang the *Liebeslieder* in London—Fräulein Thekla Friedländer and Fräulein Sophie Löwe (now Mrs. von Glehn), Fräulein Redeker (now Lady Semon), Mr. Shakespeare, and Mr. Henschel, who also sang some of the later songs for the first time.

CHAPTER III

CHARACTERISTICS OF THE ART OF BRAHMS

NO attempt to submit to a really close analysis the characteristics of a great creative artist can wholly succeed, because, even if it were possible to enumerate and catalogue the principal component parts of his work, the proportion in which they are present must for ever elude us. It would be of little service to say of a medical prescription or a culinary recipe that it contained such and such ingredients, without referring to the relative amount of each; this is all we can do in respect of works of art, and yet it must be attempted in any study of an artist's work. In the art of the composer, it will possibly be universally admitted that the most essential thing is the quality of his root-ideas, that part of his work to which the term "inspiration" is applied by fanciful, "invention" by more practical persons. It may happen, indeed, that a composer whose ideas are of the poorest and most thread-bare, may so disguise their poverty by the skill with which he places them before his hearers as to delude the world into accepting him for a time as a composer properly so called. On the other hand, a noble or distinguished musical idea may present itself to an unlearned musician, who may scarcely know how to convey it to others. Many of the most beautiful folk-songs of all nations may, nay,

BRAHMS CONDUCTING

FROM A DRAWING BY PROF. W. VON BECKERATH

must, have been derived from sources such as this, and their unknown authors deserve the name of composers far better than the other type just spoken of. But in spite of the general custom of denying to the unlettered inventor of a melody the title of musical composer so willingly granted to the clever craftsman who disguises, with gaudy orchestral colouring or remarkable contrapuntal skill, the poverty of his melodic ideas, we shall probably be justified in regarding the actual invention of melody as the first and most important of the composer's functions, and as the greatest test of his power. Next to this will come the treatment of his ideas in regard to the order of their presentation, the form and design of the music built upon them, and the process of development to which the ideas themselves are subjected. Just as in the pictorial art some kind of design, some rudimentary plan, must precede the application of colour, so the composer's treatment of form must be considered before his skill in "colouring," using that term as including the art of setting the music in the most favourable and appropriate light as regards the tone-quality of the instruments employed for its interpretation. In these days it is dangerous to imply any preference for form over colour in music, and it must not be supposed that the order in which the two are treated in the following pages is anything but an order of convenience; it is not suggested that the one is superior to the other.

(1) In the case of a very great man, it is far harder to point out the salient qualities of his work than it is with the less important men; the reason is not far to seek, nor is it very satisfactory when found, the fact being that the compositions of the latter so closely resemble others already in existence as to be capable of awakening grateful

associations in the minds of those who hear them for the first time. But the work that is not truly original must soon lose whatever distinction or freshness of appeal it ever possessed. It might safely be maintained that all the great classical masters founded their art upon the bed-rock of folk-music, that mysterious thing which seems to spring from no individual creator, but from the hearts of the people at large.

Bach, Haydn, Mozart, and Beethoven, to name no others of the great Germans, undoubtedly had the strongest admiration for the folk-music of their nation, and their most individual themes show the strongest affinity with genuine folk-song. Very frequently they used traditional themes as the basis of their works, or definitely arranged them, without reaching the level of an act of creation. No more striking instance exists of this affinity than Brahms, who arranged folk-songs for a male choir as early as 1847, whose first composition contains a folk-song as its slow movement, whose first successes out-side his native land were won by his arrangements of Hungarian dances, whose most appropriate offering to the children of his great predecessor was a set of arrange-ments of German folk-songs, and whose last published composition was a set of organ-preludes on the chorales that are the rich heritage of the Teutonic race. Apart from these, and from his great collection of actual folk-songs, published in 1894, there are abundant passages in his works of all kinds which prove how dear was traditional music to his heart. In the very earliest of his compositions, the simplicity of melodic structure that is characteristic of folk-music may not be often apparent; but as early as the B flat sextet, Op. 18, the themes strike every intelligent hearer as having the strongest affinity with the music that grows as it were spontaneously in a nation. They suggest, the first time they are heard, the idea that such beautiful and obvious sequences of notes must have been existing in the world long before they were written down; there is about them, in fact, a kind of divine familiarity such as most people can remember feeling in regard to passages of Shakespeare, when they had the impression, "But that is what I was on the point of thinking for myself!" All words that can be applied to this familiarity, whatever be the art referred to, must suggest some lack of originality; there is in reality no such lack, for in poetry the eternal truth of the idea, in the plastic art the beauty of the form and in music the essential fitness of the musical phrase, come so immediately into their own when they are read, seen, or heard, that the feeling of novelty is never realized at all. Of the great classical composers, none have surpassed Mozart, Beethoven, Schubert, and Brahms in the power of creating things that seem to have been sounding all through the ages. As Hans Sachs says—

> "Es klang so alt, und war doch so neu,
> Wie Vogelsang im süssen Mai!"

But Wagner, for all his genius, seldom managed to call forth this sudden acceptance of a new idea, and, in each of the later works especially, Brahms nearly always succeeded in doing it at least once.

From the point of view of technique this familiarity was due in great measure to his fondness for themes composed of the successive notes of a chord, those which proceed by what is called "disjunct" rather than "conjunct" motion. Though it first appears in the second of the four pianoforte ballades, it does not make itself conspicuous as a characteristic until about the date of the second symphony, whose first subject is a striking example. Another is the slow movement of the violin concerto; the songs *Feldeinsamkeit*, from Op. 86, *Sapphische Ode*, from Op. 94, and many others, contain instances that show how keenly he felt the emotional appeal that is inherent in this way of constructing themes. It seems to give a touch of intimacy, of quiet peace, almost of homeliness; were it unrelieved by themes of contrasting energy and austerity, it might easily become cloying, and it is only Brahms's masterly handling that prevents this ever being the case. The severer themes are not forced upon the attention as points of relief, and in some of the most characteristic compositions they occupy the field almost exclusively; for example, the first and last movements of the first piano concerto gave offence to the Leipzig public, no doubt because of the austerity of their themes, and even in the slow movement, exquisite as it is, there may well have seemed to the hearers in the early sixties an absence of obvious melodic beauty. An extreme instance of this austerity is the second subject of the first movement in the string quintet in G, Op. 111, but there it is to be noticed that the first subject of the same movement has a bold swing, a spirit and energy, that would have carried off a really ungainly second theme, and here there is no ungainliness, for even its asperity is so finely treated that those who know the quintet welcome it even at its first presentation, knowing what is going to be done with it. Even this asperity is rare in the later works, which for the most part are built on themes of the utmost beauty and tenderness. Perhaps the most striking examples of this are to be found in the four chamber works in which the clarinet is employed, Opp. 114, 115, and 120. The composer's admiration for the clarinet playing of Professor Mühlfeld is known to have incited him to the composition of these beautiful things; and it is not a little remarkable that they contain the only two passages in which a purist might detect something less than the ideal refinement that distinguishes all the other melodies of Brahms.

The opening of the sonata in E flat, Op. 120, No. 2, has something of what Italian critics of painting call *morbidezza*, that is, a beauty of such ripeness that the slightest touch must make it over-ripe. In the trio, Op. 114, the andantino begins with a theme that comes very near to the borders of the commonplace, for Balfe himself might (in his more inspired hours), have written something very like this :—

But whether austere or tender, all the themes of Brahms have the finest melodic curves that were ever devised in music. No man has ever attained such uniform distinction of utterance, and the presence of the two exceptions just quoted only throws into higher relief the extraordinary nobility of everything else. There is on record an intensely interesting conversation of the composer with Mr. George Henschel, in which the master analysed his own processes with rare minuteness, and in a way which must be instructive to all other composers, young or old. "What is properly called invention, or a real musical idea, is, so to say, a gift, an inspiration which I cannot further or encourage in any way (dafür kann ich nichts). At the time I must disregard this 'gift' as completely as possible, but ultimately I have to make it my own inalienable property by incessant labour. And that will not be quickly accomplished. The idea is like the seed-corn ; it grows imperceptibly in secret. When I have invented or discovered the beginning of a song such as 'Wann der silberne Mond'"—here he sang the first half-verse of *Mainacht*—"I shut up the book and go for a walk or take up something else ; I think no more of it for perhaps half a year. Nothing is lost, though. When I come back to it again, it has unconsciously taken a new shape, and is ready for me to begin working at it." [1]

(2) When we turn from the actual structure and essential features of the themes of Brahms to the manner in which he treats them, we feel ourselves in the presence of a master of the art that is called thematic development.

Never, since music was a conscious art, have the ideals of its structure been so continually fulfilled as they were by Brahms. His power of handling his materials so as to bring out every beautiful aspect of every theme, is surpassed by none of the older masters, not even by Beethoven. That power is none the less conspicuous because, for the most part, the usual types of musical form, those which are called classical, have been employed. Brahms, being in no straits for new ideas, had not the need which Liszt and other "advanced" composers had, of altering the classical forms or experimenting in new ones, for as long as he lived the old forms, so far from hampering his genius or confining his inspiration, seemed to suggest fresh outlets for development, and while there is no slavish adherence to the moulds in which Haydn and Mozart cast their thoughts, there is no opposition to the

[1] Kalbeck, ii. 178–9.

classic model. Any alteration is in the direction of amplification, the groundwork of the structure being virtually in conformity with the rules laid down long before. This is especially true of the "first-movement" form, which, in all the many examples in the work of Brahms, is identical with that used by the classical masters, though in many instances some increased interest is imparted to the regular design by the presence of a motto-theme (neither first nor second subject, but dominating both), or by incorporating part of the development with the recapitulation. A third point of great importance with Brahms is the coda, and no more striking instance of his most successful innovation in form can be pointed out than the third symphony, where the motto pervades the whole work, and the coda of the last movement introduces new matter, fusing it with the old in a manner it is impossible to forget. Sometimes, too, an extra movement is added, as the section called "Rückblick" in the piano sonata in F minor, Op. 5, or the marvellously poetic introduction to the last movement of the first symphony. In the close of the third symphony, already referred to, a touch of exquisite suggestiveness occurs quite at the end, where the first subject of the symphony (not the motto) is heard from the violins as the top note of a tremolando passage, dying down to a lovely close. The salient features of the work are discussed elsewhere (see p. 148 ff.). The coda just mentioned belongs to a class of final passages in which Brahms's genius seems to take special delight, and it has been said by an enthusiast for his work that if one might choose to have written anything by one of the great masters, one might ask to have imagined the last eight bars of each movement of the three sonatas for piano and violin, in all of which the closing strains are of rarest beauty and ingenuity. Such points as these are among the most obvious things to a student of Brahms's work, but the more deeply it is studied, the more enthusiasm will be called forth by his skill in the development of his themes, sometimes from quite unpromising germs, but more often from some melodic strain already so beautiful in itself that we might expect it to be spoilt by any process of alteration. In this special art of development we may perhaps see the highest achievement of human intellect in music. It requires not merely a complete mastery of every harmonic and contrapuntal resource, and the insight to detect in the germ of a theme its latent possibilities, but a strongly poetic invention to control the different phases of the theme, and to present them in such a succession as will enhance their beauty or eloquence. This, too, is an art that is as applicable to vocal music as to instrumental, and to the slighter forms of the romantic school as to the more conventional designs of the classical. Nothing is more remarkable throughout the work of Brahms than this splendid art, and it is perhaps not without significance that the work in which it appears for the first time in full distinctness, the finale of the piano sonata in F minor, Op. 5, should come almost immediately after one in which the composer tried the principle of "transformation of themes" which Liszt supposed himself to have invented. In the sonata in F sharp minor, Op. 2, the theme of the andante is "transformed" into that of the scherzo—a most rare expedient with Brahms, and one of which the other most prominent instance is the second symphony, Op. 73, in the appearance of the *allegretto grazioso* first in triple time in a sedate measure and then in the *presto non assai* in duple time. It is fairly clear that Brahms's adoption of the one invention claimed by the new school was never very whole-hearted, even though more instances of its employment by him might be pointed out.

For a very brief period Brahms gave in his allegiance to the school of Liszt; it is interesting to compare the episode in his social career with this momentary employment of Liszt's favourite structural device, and it is not impossible that its presence in the sonata may have induced Liszt to believe that Brahms could be regarded as a promising disciple of the new school. As usual, Joachim's words sum up the convictions of Brahms in this respect most vividly: "For him who dominates all its resources, form is no binding fetter, but a spur, an incentive, to new, free designs that are pre-eminently his own."[1] The paradox that those who make the most diligent search for new forms in music, or for new structural possibilities, are precisely those in whom the fountain of actual invention runs most slowly, and whose ideas are of the least value, is one that is being continually illustrated in modern music; and those who are richest in musical ideas are just those who find the old forms amply sufficient for their purpose.

On Brahms's treatment of rhythm a volume might be written; almost every composition of his is remarkable for its rhythmic variety, or for its superb command of metrical resources. Mr. C. F. Abdy Williams has well said, in speaking of the pianoforte *Rhapsodie*, Op. 119, No. 4, "This composition is only one amongst the many examples Brahms has given us of his mastery over rhythmical possibilities. He pushed forward the modern development of the art of music in many directions; but

[1] "Form ist ihm, der sie souverän beherrscht, keine Fessel, sondern Anregung zu immer neuen, ureigenen freien Gestaltungen" (Joachim's oration at the dedication of the Meiningen monument, 7 October, 1899).

we believe that in no direction was his work more important than in the impetus he gave to the cultivation of a high, artistic, and intellectual sense of rhythm."[1] The same author analyses many of the salient compositions of Brahms from the point of view of their rhythmic structure, and the student may well be referred to his book, which is full of interest and value.

(3) As Brahms attached so much importance to the art of design in music, it was almost inevitable that certain writers at different times should assert that he was deficient in a sense of musical "colour." The falsity of this is patent to any serious student of his work, but it is an error that has obtained a good many adherents among those who do not like his music and do not exactly know why. It is certainly true that, so far as his works give any evidence, the design of his music was of scarcely less importance than the invention of his themes, and that in his estimation the question of what instrument or tone-quality should be used in a particular passage was one of minor importance. In several cases he altered the whole scheme of colouring of a work without changing a line of its structure. The quintet, Op. 34, was originally designed for a quintet for strings, and was then turned into a sonata for two pianofortes, this latter version taking rank, not as an arrangement, but as a separate publication, numbered "Op. 34 bis." In the same way the variations on a theme by Haydn exist in two forms, "Op. 56A" being the orchestral version and "Op. 56B" that for two pianos. The vocal quartets, Op. 103, *Zigeunerlieder*, were arranged by the composer as solos with piano accompaniment, and we know enough of his independence of character to be sure that he would not do such a thing in deference to

[1] *The Rhythm of Modern Music*, p. 209.

any publisher's whim. Against these alterations of colour-scheme, to which may be added his warm approval of Joachim's adaptation for violin and piano of his arrangement of Hungarian dances originally written for piano duet, there is only a single instance in which one of his designs was afterwards modified, viz., the trio in B, Op. 8, which, first published in 1859, was reissued in 1891 with very important alterations of structure. It may be admitted, then, that he was a far more assured master of design than he was of tone-colouring; but that is not the same thing as saying that he was a bad tone-colourist, or that he had no ear for the subtle effects peculiar to the various instruments of the orchestra. Just as it is the present fashion to praise any painter who piles colour upon his canvas, and to belittle the work of the man who excels in draughtsmanship, so the public is continually being told that the whole art of music lies in piling one sonorous orchestral effect upon another; and, as it is far easier for the ear to be startled by some momentary impression of gorgeous sound, than to be trained to follow the rational development of a beautiful theme from some simple germ, the public is only too willing to follow its leaders, and to regard colour as the all-important consideration in the musical art. Where these leaders of thought got the notion that Brahms was contemptuous of musical colour, or indifferent to its charms, it is impossible to surmise; certainly it was not from the study of his music as a whole. Although in works for piano solo (to which, like most young composers, the master was limited in his earliest efforts), colour is as little to be looked for as its counterpart is in a pencil-drawing, yet in a comparison of the early sonatas and the scherzo, Opp. 1–5, with the latest piano works, Opp. 116–19, it is clear that the tone-qualities peculiar to the piano were much more fully realized in later life than in youth. As early as Op. 8, the trio in B, we meet with one passage that foreshadows many of the more individual characteristics of the later compositions. In the finale, a haunting effect of fleeting, evanescent beauty is produced by the repeated staccato notes of the violoncello subject, supported only by the light arpeggios of the piano. This use of arpeggio passages, more especially of those for piano, is of curiously frequent occurrence in the master's work, and reaches its consummation in the third symphony, where the arpeggios are given to the violins (see p. 150 f.), and the plaintive, fleeting theme to the violoncellos. Although one hesitates to suggest anything that may create a materialistic idea in connection with the work of Brahms, this characteristic idiom of his will always call up to some hearers a vision of a regretful spirit, half seen in the pale moonlight, as it flits past a scene of vanished happiness. A tearful smile, an April day, are suggested to other hearers; the point is that the effect is produced entirely by the colour-scheme. The four *Ballades*, Op. 10, contain suggestions of sonority (as in the second), or the contrast of long-held notes with an evanescent accompaniment (as in the fourth), which show that the characteristic acoustics of the piano had been closely studied. In the *Serenade*, Op. 11, in D, and in the noble *Begräbnissgesang*, Op. 13, the wind instruments are essayed for the first time, and are mostly used as Bach would have used them, that is, to carry out the design in a series of monochromes, if we may apply that word to musical tones. In the second work, the whole accompaniment is given to wind instruments, and very striking is the impression it creates, even though in England we are not apt to associate, as a

German hearer would do, the sound of wind instruments with funereal ideas. In the trios for female chorus with horns and harp, another beautiful experiment in delicate colouring was tried. It is in the two quartets for piano and strings, Opp. 25 and 26, that there is revealed for the first time that delicate and masterly handling of colour which is really peculiar to Brahms. The intermezzo of the G minor quartet, a plaintive and most spiritual movement, employs the mute for the violin, not for the other stringed instruments, and has the light treatment of the piano that has just been referred to. The andante, on the other hand, uses the stringed instruments in their most sonorous register, and the octave accompaniment of the piano is in exact balance with them. The poco adagio of the A major quartet begins with a curious device which seems to have been first used in the romance of Schumann's D minor symphony, where the solo violin and the violins of the orchestra play in what we may call approximate unison, the solo having passages of embroidery so slightly differing from the other that the casual hearer might easily infer carelessness on the part of the performers.[1] The passage is less harsh than Schumann's, because on the one hand the muted violin is so very soft, and on the other the fading tone of the piano blends the whole into an effect of great beauty. In the *Requiem* and the *Schicksalslied*, the chief stress is naturally laid, not on the thematic development of the subjects, nor on the colour employed, but on the illustration of two spiritual moods strongly contrasted with each other, the brevity and uncertainty of human life being contemplated side by side with the eternal calm of the happy dead. In the two sets of *Liebeslieder*, the

[1] See musical illustration on p. 111.

main point is the transference of the charm of the waltz to a new combination of voices and instruments. As the first piano concerto had as its main object the solution of the problem how best to combine the solo instrument with the orchestra, it is natural that we should seek in the first symphony the clear challenge of the master to the world at large as a designer and colourist at the same time. Here, no doubt, there is some ground for adverse criticism, in spite of the wonderful beauty of theme and design; the violins are kept too constantly at work, and much of the orchestration is unduly thick, so that the many felicitous touches are less prominent to the ear in performance than to the eye in reading the score. But if it contained nothing else, it would deserve distinction even among the greatest of the compositions of Brahms, by the thrilling impression created in the introduction to the finale, at a place marked *più andante*, where the horn announces a phrase against the tremolando of the muted strings. The second symphony, published only a year after the first, shows something of the same monotony and thickness of colour, but the slow movement is as rich and varied as any of the advanced school could desire. The concertos, Opp. 77 and 83, for violin and piano respectively, and the two overtures, Opp. 80 and 81, contain plenty of instances of colour dexterously used; and who that ever heard it can forget the swing of the slow movement of the violin concerto, the wit in the orchestration of the students' songs in the *Academic Overture*, or the wonderful effect of the trombones in the *Tragic?* By the date of the third symphony, Op. 90, the composer had completely realized his own ideal of scoring, and in colour the work is as fine and authoritative as it is in design. No thickness is here, but every touch tells, and makes not merely *an* effect, but *the* very effect that suits the instrument best, and best elucidates the composer's thought. The fourth symphony undoubtedly presents a stumbling-block to many of the less earnest students of the master's work, partly by the fact that its themes are presented in what we may imagine to be their primordial forms, in their very simplest and most rudimentary germs. The very square-cut rhythm of the third movement, and the adaptation of the passacaglia form to the finale, are also difficulties to the average hearer, who must hear the work very often to be able to follow the theme of the passacaglia through all its changes, and in England at the present day his chances of hearing this symphony are of the rarest. After the four symphonies, Brahms only wrote one more work in which the full orchestra is employed, the double concerto for violin and violoncello, Op. 102, in which he seems to have been mainly interested in the problem of welding together the solo instruments and the accompaniment in a new way, with entire avoidance of conventional effect.

Of colour-effects, put in for their own sake, there are very few in the concerto, but the combination of the two solo instruments (often used in a manner that suggests a string quartet) is evidently the thing which is to hold the hearer's attention, rather than the richness or variety of the orchestral background. Henceforth, the master's attention seems to have been given to the colour-possibilities of various chamber combinations, among which the group of works for clarinet, and the pianoforte solos, Opp. 116–19, are perhaps the most prominent, though the six-part choruses, Op. 104, contain many real colour-effects, such as that of the exquisite *Nachtwache II*, with its horn-like calls, "Ruh'n sie?"—"Sie ruh'n." The melancholy regret which we have referred to as being associated in Brahms's music with pianoforte arpeggios, finds its culmination in the song *Auf dem Kirchhofe*, from Op. 105. If they were nothing but studies in colouring, the pianoforte pieces of the later period would deserve immortality, so varied are the moods suggested in the mere disposition of the special keyboard effects, quite apart from the enthralling interest of the thematic invention and development.

It has seemed worth while to labour this point of the relation of Brahms's music to colour, since colour is more thought of than anything else by amateur and professional critics in the present day. When the art of design regains its old place in general estimation, it is certain that the position of Brahms among the supreme masters of music will be even more widely acknowledged than it is at present by the world at large.

BRAHMS AT THE PIANO

FROM A DRAWING BY PROF. W. VON BECKERATH

CHAPTER IV

THE PIANOFORTE WORKS

LIKE all ardent young composers, Brahms must needs at first express himself with the means that were easily at his disposal, and, as usually happens, his first conceptions were allotted to the pianoforte, and after making a beginning with this instrument, songs followed next. There was an additional reason in his case for writing his earliest works for the piano, since it was the instrument he himself had studied, and on which he was a more or less finished performer before the eventful day on which he presented himself to Joachim.[1]

Among the compositions with which he was provided in 1853, were a violin sonata (the one that was afterwards lost), a trio-fantasia, and other things, but certainly the piano sonatas, Opp. 1 and 2, the scherzo, Op. 4, and the first set of songs, Op. 3. Of this early batch of works, those which have been published are far more interesting to the student than are the usual run of youthful compositions, even when these proceed from one afterwards accepted as a great man. They show us with wonderful clearness at what point Brahms stood with regard alike to pianoforte technique and to formal methods

[1] As late as 1887 he felt more at ease in writing for the piano than for any other instrument. See *Joachim Correspondence*, ii. 226.

of construction. In the former respect, they contain things which no piano can possibly realize to the full; the handfuls of chords, though they demand hands of great size and strength, yet do not represent all the mass of sound which the young composer wants, only all that he could get from one pair of hands. The phase of technique which the sonatas illustrate is that of the school where muscular force ranked highest, where gradation of tone was less regarded than strong contrasts, and where the art of *cantabile* playing was a little at a discount. Not that the sonatas are without opportunities for *cantabile*; but a player who had little power of "singing" on the keyboard, but who could produce a large volume of tone, would succeed in them quite as well as a more sensitive interpreter. The contrasts are less those of different qualities of tone than of mere force, and they derive their chief interest from their inherent rightness, not from the richness of their colour. It used to be said that the early pianoforte works of Brahms were not real piano music; this is by no means true, for even in the first sonatas there are passages that lie well for the hands (as well as some that lie more or less ill). The end of the first movement of the first sonata can never be really very effective, but as a rule the sonorities of the instrument are well considered. Opinions differ greatly as to the characteristics of Brahms's own playing, and it seems, in fact, to have varied at various times of his life. Joachim's eulogy has been already quoted (see p. 6), and Miss May describes it in detail and with enthusiasm; but Madame Schumann writes of it with almost unqualified disapproval.[1] Two anecdotes are given by Kalbeck,[2] which illustrate, as the writer carefully points out, the richness and beautiful

[1] Litzmann, *Clara Schumann*, iii. 218, etc.

[2] i. 227.

quality of his tone. Once, when Brahms was playing at the Schumanns', Frau Schumann came into the room and asked, "Who was that playing duets?" A child, the daughter of a famous singer who was buying a new grand piano, said, "Herr Brahms must play on that; he never does a piano any harm, he only strokes it."

In regard to structure and form, we must suppose that Brahms had imbibed the conventions of the classical design from Marxsen; the commonplace view of the composer is that he was all his life bound by the rules of form, that he would have done better to obey his inspiration rather than to follow the lead of the stricter classical masters, and that his imagination, unfettered by any considerations of design, would have found more spontaneous utterance. If those who use such *clichés* of criticism would pay a little attention to the early sonatas, they would see reason to modify opinions which have nothing to recommend them but the fact that they have obtained a wide acceptance. The opening theme of the sonata in C, Op. 1 (appropriately dedicated, on its publication, to Joachim), bears an obvious likeness to the beginning of the "Hammerclavier" sonata of Beethoven and the "Wandererfantasie" of Schubert, but it is only a surface resemblance, and the masterly development of the second subject is enough to prove the young composer's complete assimilation of the orthodox rules. In the finale, the opening theme appears in a new guise, transformed after the manner of Liszt. Perhaps it may be well to remind the general reader of the so-called invention which Liszt proposed to substitute for the logical development of the subjects after the classical model. That model derives its main interest, after the two chief subjects have been stated, from a course of treatment known as "working-out," in which every freedom is permitted the composer to vary the aspect of the themes as he may please. Very often in the hands of a great master of this "development," a theme which at first seems unpromising, angular, or inadequate to take the chief part in a movement, is so developed as to become a thing of unforgettable beauty before the movement is done. But this process is one of the greatest tests of a composer's powers, for whereas convention and second-hand learning may help him to present his two subjects in the orthodox way, it is in the development section that his imagination is most surely set free.

To those who possess no musical imagination, or whose means of expressing what they have are deficient, this section must always present unconquerable difficulties; even Schubert was not always completely successful here, and the flounderings of Chopin do much to spoil the first movements of both his sonatas and of his trio. Liszt and his friends, loud in the denunciation of the classical forms, and eager to find an alternative system of design, lit upon the idea of altering the themes not by a gradual process, but by sudden changes of rhythm or aspect; the "transformation of themes," as the principle was called, implied the continuance of a certain small number of themes through several movements, and the successive presentment of them in changed aspects in each. No attempt was made at real development, and the newer system seemed at one time to hold in it possibilities of new forms, and to give opportunities to composers whose imaginative powers were weak. We are not now concerned to trace the futility of the system down to more modern days; when still newer principles of design are seen to run through the compositions of the more modern writers, it is not likely that Liszt's example will be followed for much longer.

Even down to the present day the classical system has prevailed with all the more earnest composers of each country, with the possible exception of César Franck, who adopted a principle of his own, not identical with either of the others.

Brahms, then, tried his hand at the "Liszt" system of "transformation," making the theme of the finale of this first sonata from that of the first movement, and presenting it in a new rhythm, in which we are prevented from feeling how sterile it is in this form, because there are such beautiful subordinate themes in the movement. One, in A minor, $\frac{6}{8}$ time, was a deliberate reference, as Brahms told Dietrich, to the theme of the song, *Mein Herz ist im Hochland.*[1] Another case of the same kind of "transformation" treatment occurs in a less obvious way after the slow movement—a kind of fantasia on the volkslied, *Verstohlen geht der Mond auf*[2]—which ends in an exquisitely tender and truly romantic passage on a tonic pedal; a cadence-phrase in the last bar gives the suggestion for the vigorous theme of the scherzo.

The sonata in F sharp minor, Op. 2, has a splendidly energetic first subject, but the second theme is almost too much in the manner of Schumann, possibly with intention, as the piece was dedicated to that composer's wife. The

theme of the *andante* reminds one of the folk-song

[1] It is difficult to say what setting of Burns's words is here referred to; the theme is not that of the tune to which Burns wrote them, nor is it that of Schumann's song.

[2] It is interesting to compare the version of the tune here given, with the version in the last (choral) book of *Deutsche Volkslieder*, where the third line is different from the first, and various harmonic variations are also to be traced.

of the first sonata, and from Dietrich we learn that here again the old song beginning *Mir ist leide* gave the suggestion.[1] It is "transformed" into this phrase for

the scherzo, a movement of curious beauty, relieved by an exquisitely calm trio in a mood that Brahms was often to repeat. It has a kind of rusticity about it that could not be anything but German. The type is set in the seventh variation of Bach's "Goldberg" series, and could be traced in many places in Schubert, notably in the minuet-trio of the fantasia-sonata in G.

The finale, introduced by a very effective piece of pianoforte rhetoric, is on a bold subject, "developed" in such a way as to show the far greater possibilities which Brahms seems to find in the classical system than in the later method. A series of long chords, just after the double-bar, has a strangely beautiful and "atmospheric" effect, and the movement rises to a fine climax at the introduction of the main theme in augmentation, and in octaves, *fortissimo*, after which the work quietly ends, the subdued brilliance of its final passage looking, on the one hand, back to the close of Chopin's *Barcarole*, and, on the other, forward to the similar ending of César Franck's *Prélude, Aria, et Final.*

The next of these early works, the scherzo in E flat minor, Op. 4, carries us again back to Chopin, whose four scherzos might be supposed to have been the model on which it was built (but see p. 6); although they run on consecutively, there is just as real a differentiation between

[1] Kalbeck, i. 221.

the main theme and the contrasting sections as there is between Brahms's vigorous main theme and the two trios which are so finely contrasted with it and with each other. The scherzo was actually written before either of the sonatas, but, as Brahms said to Louise Japha, " When one shows oneself for the first time, people must first see the head and not the feet."[1] No wonder that Liszt, judging by the works that Brahms took him, should have hailed him as a " modern " in embryo, in sympathy with the romantic Chopin, and ready to adopt Liszt's pet device of " transformation." It is clear to us nowadays that that device was never very dear to Brahms, and in the third sonata, in F minor, Op. 5, we can almost see him in the act of using transformation for the last time as a deliberate means of extending the movement. In the finale, a theme which appears at first as a subordinate subject in D flat gradually usurps attention, until with an increase of speed and a diminution of the note-values, it is transformed from a stately chorale-like tune to a brilliant presto for the peroration. But in the first movement there is development and logical working out of thematic material presented in the orthodox way. Kalbeck[2] finds in the theme in A flat a reminiscence of Elsa's "dream," and the main phrase in the exquisite conclusion of the slow movement is undoubtedly identical with a prominent phrase in Hans Sachs's soliloquy in Act II of *Die Meistersinger*, "Dem Vogel, der heut' sang." The first might conceivably have been a remembrance, conscious or unconscious, but if the second is anything but a pure coincidence, the charge of plagiarism cannot be established against Brahms, whose sonata was published thirteen years before *Die Meistersinger* was composed. The movement, which is of exquisitely lyrical quality, has

[1] Kalbeck, i. 224. [2] i. 225–6.

a quotation from Sternau describing evening, and after the vigorous scherzo—a movement suggesting Mendelssohn in its theme[1]—the short section called *Rückblick* gathers up again the theme of the andante and presents it in a guise suggesting a funeral march. Of the three sonatas this is the most often played in the present day, for it is technically very effective, and its poetry is easy to understand and to interpret.

The next work for pianoforte solo, Op. 9, consists of a set of variations on a theme of Robert Schumann, in F sharp minor. The fourth piece in that master's *Bunte Blätter*, Op. 90, is called *Albumblatt*, and during his last illness Frau Schumann composed variations on it. During her convalescence after the birth of her seventh child, Brahms wrote a set of variations to amuse her, and submitted each one to her as it was written.[2] The set has many personal allusions to the Schumann household, and seems to be deliberately cast in a Schumannesque mould, as if more were suggested than was actually uttered. The first variation uses the theme as a bass; in the third it appears in an inner part; its first three notes suggest variations 7 and 8, and for number 9 (in which the key is changed for the first time), the pattern of another piece of Schumann's, a little composition that immediately follows that on which the variations are built (viz., Op. 99, No. 5) is taken for the figure. The tenth of the series is a masterpiece of interweaving different themes, and the resulting effect is strikingly beautiful, whether we analyse its structure or not. As a matter of

[1] The finale of Mendelssohn's C minor trio must have been unconsciously based on Legrenzi's song, *Che fiero costume*, which thus becomes the ultimate original of this beautiful movement of Brahms.

[2] Miss May's *Life*, i. 160.

fact the original bass of the theme is put at the top, appearing in the key of D major, but unaltered in notes; a new bass is made by inverting the intervals of the original bass, upon the supertonic of the scale as a centre, so that the E of the new key in either part is answered by E, D by F sharp, C sharp by G, and so on. Between these two extremities the theme of the variations appears in notes of one-quarter the original value:—

Even this does not exhaust the wonders of the variation, for near its close, three bars from the end, we hear the characteristic notes of a theme by Frau Schumann (*Romance Variée*, Op. 3), upon which Schumann had long before written variations, they being his Opus 5. The greatest marvel of all in this tenth variation of Brahms's work is its deeply emotional power; from this point onwards the poetical imagination of the young man bears all before it until in the last three we find ourselves in a world of romance, where even Schumann's mysticism is surpassed. The last variation, with its faint, suspended harmonies, on the bass of the theme, dies away into silence with magical effect.[1]

The curious and beautiful work, Op. 10, which follows

[1] The student should refer to what Brahms says about the different variation-forms in the *Herzogenberg Correspondence*, i. 8 (trans., 8).

the Schumann variations immediately, is sometimes spoken of as if it were really a sonata, though it has few of the sonata characteristics, except the close relation of its keys. The four *Balladen* may very possibly have been suggested by Herder's *Stimmen der Völker* (a work to which the composer again had recourse in one of his latest piano pieces), and the first has the grim force of the Scottish *Edward*, the words of which were afterwards used in Op. 75, No. 1; but it is not in sonata-form, and Brahms was far too true a lover of that form to use the name without conforming to its laws. The second ballade is a pure lyric, one of the loveliest slow movements ever written for piano, and true piano-music in every bar. The spreading notes of the andante,[1] the vigour of the allegro, the elfin beauty of the notes sustained, in the middle section, against the fleeting sounds in the right hand, the resumption of the first strain in a new key, bringing one back to the original key quite naturally, all these are points that must appeal to every player and hearer. The "intermezzo," No. 3, reminds us of the Chopinesque scherzo, Op. 4, but the weird, archaic beauty of the section in the relative major is more poetical than anything in the earlier work. The fourth ballade, after its Schubertian waverings between minor and major, strikes the same mysterious note in the *più lento*, when the composer deliberately orders that the melody in an inner part is not to be too definitely marked, and reaches a close of rare suggestiveness and beauty, in which the two themes are finely worked together. We feel under the influence of the mystic side of Schumann's fantasia, Op. 17, at its close.

[1] Kalbeck (i. 102) points out that these notes, F, A, F, stand for "Frei, aber froh," a motto chosen by Brahms as a counterpart to the "Frei, aber einsam" of Joachim. See p. 49.

Before the next pianoforte solos, the composer had made several excursions into the field of orchestral writing, and had lived down the chorus of execration with which the piano concerto in D minor had been received. Two sets of variations make up Op. 21, both in D major, the first on an original theme, consisting of two nine-bar strains of $\frac{3}{8}$ time, and the second on a Hungarian song of $\frac{7}{4}$ time (treated as alternate bars of $\frac{3}{4}$ and common time); the first set was played by Frau Schumann at the Gewandhaus in 1860 (the year before publication). The variations follow one another in wonderful logical sequence, the first two being built on an ornamental form of the theme used as a bass, the next pair presenting the essential harmonies with suspensions, No. 5 being a canon in contrary motion, of an emotional depth as great as its contrapuntal skill, and the seventh giving the effect of extraordinary harmonic complexity, though only two parts are employed. The vigorous movement started in the eighth variation quiets down in the tenth to a long bass shake in the eleventh, which refers to the figures of several of the other variations. The allusion, near the close of the series, to the phrase of Schubert's *Wanderer*—"Dort, wo du nicht bist, dort ist das Glück"—is obviously intentional, but no explanation of it is given in the biographies. The second set, on a Hungarian song, is much more of a bravura piece than the first, and ends with a regular finale, the bustling figure of which is gradually developed from the point when the septuple time is abandoned in variation nine. Only the choral *Marienlieder* separate these from two more sets of variations, the first for pianoforte duet on a theme of Schumann, the second on a subject from Handel's second book of suites, where it is already made a subject for variations. The theme of Schumann is the pathetic melody by which the composer was haunted about three weeks before his mind gave way. He was actually engaged upon variations on the theme at the time of the attempted suicide in the Rhine. He was convinced that the spirit of Schubert had sung it to him. The first four of Brahms's variations are like a summary of certain favourite devices of Schumann, the gloomy fourth leading us into the older master's most intimate mood; in the fifth we have the true Brahms in a pastoral vein (compare this with the nineteenth and twenty-second of the Handel set, or the intermezzo of the G minor quartet, Op. 25), the sixth recalls us to active life, and the little solo, after the vaguely alternating harmonies of the beginning of No. 7, seems to suggest an orchestral effect as of an oboe or clarinet. The strenuous mood of the ninth has a noble transition to the tenth, a funeral march of obvious significance, and the coda resumes the theme in altered guise.

The "Handel" variations, Op. 24, for piano solo, begin in a matter-of-fact and Handelian style, but soon a deeper emotion comes in. In Nos. 3–6 a new theme is generated from the old, and the texture of the work becomes closer and richer; the "largamente," No. 13, is a splendidly impressive elegy; and Nos. 23–25 work up a forcible climax to the entry of the fugue, which fits the concert-room better than the study, and has a wonderfully effective dominant pedal near the end. The whole series, as a subsidiary matter, shows the pianoforte technique of Brahms's earlier years to perfection, and it is not surprising that it was not often played until the average virtuoso's skill had advanced to a point where the difficulties of these variations are part of his ordinary day's work.

An even higher grade of technique is required in the two books[1] of variations on a theme of Paganini, Op. 35. The theme, which is No. 24 of Paganini's *Capricci*, Op. 1, and has variations of its own, consists of little more than a sequence of harmonies such as is most prolific in suggestion to the skilful variation writer. Bach's great "Goldberg" series of thirty variations for harpsichord, his "Chaconne" for violin alone, and Beethoven's thirty-two variations in C minor, are the greatest examples of this kind of treatment of the harmonic basis of the theme. A certain number of the variations by Brahms seem to have been suggested by Paganini's own variations, and in the transcription of Weber's *moto perpetuo* with the functions of the two hands interchanged, in the two versions of a certain presto of Bach, and in the transcription of the same master's *Chaconne* (for left hand alone) Brahms, it is clear, took a delight in translating one kind of difficulty into its equivalent. Nos. 1 and 13 of the first book show the influence of Paganini's second variation, the finale of the same set has a figure which appears in Paganini's finale, and No. 8 of Brahms's second book is an enlargement of Paganini's first variation. These are, notwithstanding, perfectly original in spirit, and such things as 6, 9, 12, the last of the first book, 2, 4, and 7 of the second, and the last of all the 28, are purest Brahms, although in musical interest and importance the series may not compare with many of the other sets of variations.

The piano-duet form again attracted Brahms, and in Op. 39 he wrote for four hands a set of sixteen waltzes,

[1] The division into two books seems to have worried Madame Schumann. See Litzmann, *Clara Schumann*, iii. 178, where she states her preference for the finale of the first book, and suggests various changes of sequence, etc.

some of which he had composed several years before the completion of the set. They are quite as effective for two hands as for four, and the elasticity of their rhythm can be better preserved in the solo than in the duet. Like the *Liebeslieder*, they are really "ländler" rather than waltzes, but all of them might be called "Soirées de Vienne," though they were written before Brahms took up his residence in Vienna. The theme of No. 5 was used for a vocal quartet, *Der Gang zur Liebsten*, Op. 31, No. 3, which appeared before the waltzes but was written after them. There are many lovely things in the waltzes, and nothing is stranger than their quiet ending; after the stress of Nos. 13 and 14, when the exquisite and familiar little strain in A flat is over, there is in the final waltz a piece of double counterpoint as much unsuspected by the average hearer as a similar device in the quartet in Act II of *Figaro;* a curious thing about the waltz is that the second strain of it is just as much in double counterpoint as the first, but it is not exhibited with the parts inverted, the section being repeated literally.

Though the quintet, Op. 34, appeared as a duet for two pianos, and the "Haydn" variations similarly disposed count as a separate opus number, not as a transcription of an orchestral piece, yet it will be best to consider the former among the chamber compositions and the latter among the orchestral, seeing that the ultimate disposition of both is fixed by general consent and the master's own decision.

We pass on to the eight *Clavierstücke*, Op. 76, and the two *Rhapsodies*, Op. 79, which complete the composer's works for piano solo down to the latest period, when the all-important Opp. 116–9 delighted the world. It seems as though in regard to short piano pieces Brahms was in doubt as to the names they should bear, so that while the non-committal "Clavierstücke" pledged him to nothing, the name "Capriccio" was bestowed on the rapid pieces, and "Intermezzo" on the slower, "Rhapsodie" being reserved for the two pieces Op. 79. In truth there is nothing very rhapsodical about these last, nor any trace of caprice about the "Capricci"; the "Intermezzi" appear to be intended for separate use, not as intervening between two other compositions, so that the whole set of pieces might seem to be wrongly named. But whatever their titles, it is undeniable that the eight pieces of Op. 76 have a high value of their own, to the general student as to the professed "Brahmsianer." Though Nos. 1, 5, and 8 seem to be taken up with the working of groups of quavers with free use of the cross-rhythms which come of viewing them as twice three or three times two, the three pieces are very different in emotional purport; the first has some of the chilling atmosphere of the wind-swept churchyard in the song, *Auf dem Kirchhofe;* the fifth, in its presentment of a persistent striving after some desired object, is in rather a new mood for Brahms, although his way of working two against three is familiar; and the eighth is joyous and eminently graceful. The second, the well-known staccato piece in B minor, needs no eulogium, and the third, with its strange acoustic effects produced by sustaining the thin high chords upon a fleeting accompaniment, produces an impression quite new to piano music. The fourth, with the inverted arpeggios of its accompaniments, is a prophecy of the later piece in which the device is pushed to its furthest limits (Op. 119, No. 1); No. 6, in spite of a similarity of theme to Beethoven's "andante favori" in F, is a real relief in its place (compare its middle section with that of Op. 118, No. 2), and No. 7 has the suppressed energy of an old ballad. Energy, neither suppressed nor wasted, is the note of the two *Rhapsodies*, Op. 79, though the musette-like trio of the first, and the mysterious pianissimo passage in the second, hide that energy for a time; in the second the gradual slackening of the triplet figure seems to indicate that the object is attained rather than that the striver's strength is spent.

It would be absurd to suppose that the four sets of piano pieces which appeared in 1892-3 were written shortly before their publication; probably some of them were actually conceived at any time after the issue of the two *Rhapsodies*, *i.e.*, between 1880 and 1892. The delicate lyrical character of many of them would not have served for movements of the greater works upon which the composer was engaged during those years, and there is no doubt that he felt them to suit the character of the piano better than any other instrument. Though not less difficult of execution than any of the earlier pieces, they are far more grateful to the player, and far more "playable." It is all piano music of the highest quality. The impression they created on a sympathetic admirer like Madame Schumann is recorded in her diary.[1]

Op. 116, called *Fantasien*, begins with a vigorous presto in D minor with difficult accentuations; in No. 2 we strike a vein of gentle pathos that is worked in many of these pieces for the first time; No. 3 is a masterpiece of pianoforte sonority, and the middle section in E flat has one of the most irresistible tunes in the whole of Brahms. In the fourth, an "intermezzo" in E major, there is a subtle touch showing how fully the composer understood what is a really typical effect of the piano; between the deeply

[1] Litzmann's *Clara Schumann*, iii. 563, etc.

expressive, even passionate, phrases of the melody at the top, are little *ritornelli*, in which the right hand has to cross over, rather pointlessly, as a superficial student might think, to play the bass notes; by thus obliging the left hand to play the uppermost part for the moment, there is almost inevitably produced a kind of dull tone, which is exactly what Brahms wants as a colour-contrast. The whole of this little piece, the use of the soft pedal, the simultaneous employment of chords played with and without arpeggio, and the disposal of the chords, would be enough to prove that Brahms was fully sensible of what is called "colour" in music. The intermezzo in E minor, No. 5, is one of the less obvious of his works, but its suggested suspensions, and the flowing legato of its middle part, endear it to his professed admirers. No. 6, a perfect minuet in form, is again called "Intermezzo," that name sharing with "Capriccio" the titles of the pieces called collectively *Fantasies*, showing that the names meant little or nothing to the composer. No. 7 is a wild and rhapsodical piece with a central melody, each note of which is delayed, after the manner of some pieces of Schumann.

The first of the three "Intermezzi," Op. 117, carries an inscription from Herder's *Volkslieder*, which serves to identify the German poem with *Lady Anne Bothwell's Lament*, beginning "Baloo, my babe." It is an exquisitely simple lullaby, with a touch of dark foreboding in its middle section. In No. 2 we recognize that pathetic use of the arpeggio which was noted as one of the most salient characteristics of Brahms's music. It is not claimed that there is anything new in the figure, or in the manner of its employment, but in the spiritual application (as it may be called) of the musical device to describe a mental state that cannot be put into words there is something emphatically new. In this case, the figure suggests a chilling autumn wind that, as it blows the dead leaves to and fro, calls up feelings of a regret that is scarcely painful for some long-past happiness. There is no foreboding here, as there is in a later piano piece, in the finale of the A major violin sonata, or in the slow movement of the pianoforte quartet, Op. 26; nor is the resultant impression quite as ethereal and fairy-like as is that of the *poco allegretto* of the third symphony. But if less poignant, the sorrowful element seems to lie deeper and to be more human than it is in either of the other movements. The third of the series is in the mood of some old ballad, and its romantic middle section may suggest some wayward spirit of the woodland, some Lorelei or Undine.

The intermezzo with which Op. 118 begins is slightly touched with the plaintive spirit we associate with Brahms's arpeggios, but it is rather a prelude to the happy intimacy of the next following piece, the intermezzo in A, than an independent work. The ballade which comes third is the most vigorous in outward form of all the later pieces, and the contrasting quietude of the middle portion sets its virility in a brilliant light. In No. 4 Brahms sets us a puzzle, which most of the pianists of the day seem to regard as hopeless of solution. But if they would emphasize the notes to which an accent is attached, they could hardly fail to see that it is a study built on the descent of an octave, everything in the melodic part, whether single notes or passages, being immediately reiterated an octave below, generally with altered harmony. Sometimes, as a natural result of this, short canonic passages occur, but their presence need not alarm those to whom such things are an abomination, for it is never obtruded. The principle of repetition an octave below gives rise to a beautiful figure in the middle part, and is carried through to the very end with extraordinary determination. The next piece, the "romance" in F, is infinitely gracious in effect (that the two strains of its first part are in double counterpoint is best left unnoticed), and the series of *fioriture* on a pedal D gives to the *allegretto grazioso* a touch of virtuosity that makes the piece beloved of those who can perform it. No. 6, in E flat minor, yet another intermezzo, is perhaps the most significant and poetic of all the later pieces. A wailing little phrase that might be executed on an oboe is answered by a harp-like passage, full of menace, and the two are worked together up to a climax of irresistible power. There is a savage triumph in the new theme then introduced, which puts the other subjects out of sight for a short time, but the wailing theme, re-entering while the climax is in progress, finally asserts itself and closes the piece in a grandly tragic way. The work is dramatically eloquent, as it could not be if there were a "programme" appended to it; it could not be as vivid if the plot of *Macbeth* or *Lear* were associated with it, and it may stand as a permanent refutation of the heresy that music to be alive must illustrate something outside music.

The first piece of Op. 119 is worked on a scheme of descending thirds which make up what the English theorist, Day, called chords of the eleventh; in spite of a middle theme of rare loveliness and winning grace, the piece is not for every one to play or listen to. The next begins in an agitated manner, with a theme of which we do not suspect the possibilities till it appears in the major, as a "ländler" of bewitching beauty. The dainty intermezzo in C, with its undercurrent of melody and the continual play of its reiterated notes above, is like some skilfully contrived fountain; just before the resumption of the theme, and again at the end, there is a little gust of wind that suggests the wisdom of stepping backwards so as not to be wetted with the spray. The last of the set, and Brahms's last work for piano alone, is called *Rhapsodie.* It has more thematic material, and is more elaborate as well as more brilliant than the others; it marches along with a great swing at first, and the introduction of a triplet figure does not impede its progress or alter its step; a charming melody, that could not be imagined on any other instrument than the piano, serves as "trio," and the march reaches a noble climax afterwards, with final passages of great difficulty such as appeal to the ordinary virtuoso. It is noteworthy that Brahms, here and in one other work, has broken through a certain convention; while the minor compositions of old times were always made to end in the major, with what was called a *tierce de Picardie*, it was most rare, then and later, to end a major composition in the minor. This *Rhapsodie* begins in E flat major, and the whole trend of it is towards a conclusion in that key, but the coda insists on a minor close for some reason or other at which we cannot guess.[1]

The fifty-one *Uebungen*, which actually appeared after Op. 119, had no doubt been devised long before, and are properly classed with Brahms's curious experiments in transcription, which have been already mentioned. They are wholly mechanical so far as having next to no melodic idea, and in regard to the unchanging figure of each; but the little "etc." with which a large number of them conclude demands exceptional powers of transposi-

[1] Compare the trio, Op. 8, which has a minor close to its finale. See p. 108.

tion and resource on the part of the student, who must play these things a semitone higher at each repetition. In the mere matter of technique the *Uebungen* have no very great importance. Odd little expedients, such as practised pianists meet with but once or twice in a lifetime, are here made the subject of elaborate exercises, and many of the others are calculated to tire rather than to train the artist's fingers. The composer's command of pianoforte technique is shown to be far more complete and far more truly sympathetic with the instrument in the later piano pieces, Opp. 116–19, than in these exercises. The arrangements, some of which have been referred to above, include Chopin's F minor study set in sixths, Weber's "moto perpetuo" with the right-hand part adapted for the left, two versions of a presto of Bach from the first unaccompanied violin sonata in G, his chaconne arranged for left hand alone, Gluck's gavotte in A from *Paride ed Elena* arranged for the special use of Madame Schumann, and twenty-one *Ungarische Tänze*, two books of which appeared in 1869 and two more in 1880. Originally set for four hands on the piano, the first two books were arranged for piano solo by the composer in 1872; and in Joachim's arrangements for piano and violin the dances have preserved their popularity to the present day. The themes of the great majority [1] are taken from the stores of national Hungarian csárdás, and are to be heard from every Hungarian band; but the spirit with which the characteristics of the Hungarian performers are caught and transferred to the pianoforte is irresistible, and it will be long before the dances are forgotten or Brahms's name dissociated from them. There exists also an arrangement by Brahms of Schumann's quartet for piano and strings as a piano duet,

[1] Some are original. See Kalbeck, i. 66.

as well as an edition of Handel's vocal chamber duets with piano accompaniment, a model of what such things should be. The complete edition of Couperin enjoyed the value of his co-operation; and he was also concerned in those brought out by Breitkopf and Härtel of the complete works of Schumann and Chopin. It is not generally known that he filled up the figured bass, in the two beautiful sonatas for piano and violin, by C. P. E. Bach, which Rieter-Biedermann published some years ago. An orchestral version of the accompaniment to some of Schubert's songs, among them *Greisengesang*, *Geheimes*, and *Memnon*, was also made; the effect of these hardly came up to the master's expectation, but two others, *An Schwager Kronos* and *Gruppe aus dem Tartarus*, were given with great effect by the Vienna Gesangverein, with the vocal part sung by all the men of the chorus.

The Organ Works

Three works for organ solo may be more conveniently considered here than elsewhere. In 1864 the *Allgemeine Musikalische Zeitung* contained as a supplement an organ fugue in the startling key of A flat minor. Whether the seven flats in the signature deterred the average organist from the piece, or not, we cannot say, but the fugue has never acquired the vogue which Brahms's name might have ensured for it. In 1881 the *Musikalisches Blatt* included a chorale-vorspiel and fugue on "O Traurigkeit, O Herzeleid," the subject of the fugue being suggested by, rather than founded on, the chorale-melody. It is a curious coincidence that both these fugues have their answers at first by inversion. Both were among the compositions dating from the time when Brahms and

Joachim exchanged their works for mutual help and criticism.

Far more important than either of these, though some of them date from the same period, is the set of eleven Chorale-vorspiele or Preludes, which were the only compositions left behind at the master's death. The majority of them were written at Ischl in the summer of 1896, and all were published in 1902. Here are examples of both the approved styles of setting chorales, notably that of which Bach was so fond, in which a figure derived from the hymn-tune is worked before the entrance, and between the lines, of the chorale, during the long pauses which, originally made for the convenience of the congregation, have borne such a rich harvest of artistic results. Of such treatment are No. 1, *Mein Jesu, der du mich* (canto fermo in the pedal part), No. 4, *Herzlich thut mich erfreuen* (canto fermo in treble), No. 7, *O Gott, du frommer Gott* (canto fermo, first in treble, then in bass and finally in treble), and No. 10, *Herzlich thut mich verlangen (ii)* (canto fermo in pedal).

In another class, the pauses between the lines are ignored (in the case of *Schmücke dich* the player must ignore them even though they are printed above the notes, as their presence is meant merely as a guide to the disposition of the lines of the hymn), and the hymn-tune is presented often in an ornate version, but without interludes, or with only very short interludes. No. 2, *Herzliebster Jesu*, No. 3, *O Welt, ich muss dich lassen (i)*, No. 5, *Schmücke dich, o liebe Seele*, No. 6, *O wie selig*, No. 8, *Es ist ein Ros' entsprungen*, and No. 9, *Herzlich thut mich verlangen (i)*, are examples of this style of treatment. In all these the chorale-tune is in the treble part, as it is also in the most beautiful and expressive of the set, No. 11, *O Welt, ich muss dich lassen (ii)*, in which each line is followed by a kind of double echo effect, arranged to be played on three manuals, the second echo repeating only a part of the first. Beautiful as they are on the organ, there are yet instances when some other medium, not the organ, seems required for their perfect realization.

This is especially true of the tenth and eleventh ; in the tenth, the reiterated notes of the bass, on the manual, do not tell as reiterated notes, unless so light a stop is used that insufficient support is given to the melody in the pedal part. For this a more beautiful effect is obtained if a baritone voice sings the words of the hymn, and the manual-parts are played on the pianoforte, as in the case of Bach's exquisite chorale-prelude, *Erbarm' dich mein, o Herre Gott*, where the same balance creates the same practical difficulty. In the last bars of No. 11 the gradual fading away of the last echo cannot be properly expressed on the organ, where the middle part, carrying the melody, cannot be brought out, nor its notes given the small emphasis they seem to require; but the pianoforte cannot fail to give exactly the effect it may be supposed the master wanted. It is an open question whether he was not thinking more of the piano than of the organ in writing these two, if no others of the set. Was ever so suitable an ending to any human work achieved as this eleventh chorale-prelude ? As the melody fades away, we seem to catch a glimpse of the soaring spirit entering into its rest and reward.

CHAPTER V

CONCERTED MUSIC

IF we allowed ourselves to feign a total annihilation of all the music of Brahms with the exception of one single class of his work, we should be probably justified in thinking that the class chosen by the world in general for preservation would be the concerted chamber music. It is this which first awoke the passionate love for his art in the souls of many English people, and although the violin sonata, which was among the pieces shown to Schumann, has been lost beyond hope of recovery, yet we know that Schumann was as much impressed by it as by any of the other compositions. Of course, if it could be shown that the universal vote would be for this class against all the rest, that would prove absolutely nothing one way or the other as to its relative merits, as compared with the other branches of music in which so many masterpieces were left. But such a vote would demonstrate the popularity of this class, and the general opinion that in this Brahms excelled more incontestably than elsewhere. The forms of ensemble music for instruments are apt to find out the weak places in the equipment of those whose aim is chiefly colour, and who naturally rejoice in the chances they get when writing for the orchestra. A great designer, as distinguished from a great colourist, will feel more at home, and be apt to do his best work in monochrome, and there are masters whose pencil drawings are far more valuable than their finished oil pictures. Although we may not desire to give support to the stupid assertion that Brahms was not a fine colourist, we may be willing to admit that noble design was more to him than the most skilful colour-scheme. It is significant of the unity of purpose which marked all the work of the great composer from beginning to end that the earliest piece of his ensemble work now extant, published after his death, should yet not seem unworthy of his maturest days. The single movement which he contributed to the violin sonata written jointly with Schumann and Albert Dietrich, is the short scherzo in D minor, Dietrich having provided the first movement and Schumann the intermezzo and finale. This was published with Joachim's permission some years after the death of Brahms, in 1906.

The scherzo is unmistakably the work of one who was destined to do great things in the world, though as yet it might have seemed uncertain whether he would keep to the old-established forms or break out into experiments of doubtful success. It starts with reiterated notes on the violin alone, and the rise of a semitone with which the piano part begins is soon—but not till after the repeat of the first part—developed into a flowing phrase in which the upward and downward leap of an octave is a prominent feature. The trio begins with a new melodic phrase which promises excellently ; but after fourteen bars it is evident that the composer is hankering again after the figures of the scherzo, and after uniting them with the trio phrase, the scherzo is definitely resumed, the trio phrase serving for an almost operatic coda. This movement would, of course, not have been enough to assure Brahms's position among the great masters, but even from it alone there was to be discerned the promise of future eminence.

The first concerted piece with an opus-number is the trio for piano and strings, in B major, Op. 8, the work by which the name of Brahms was introduced to the United States as early as 1855. Here, too, is a striking example of the unity of ideals and aims which lasted all through the master's life; for there is surely no other instance of a great and accepted master going back to one of his earliest works, and revising it in such a way that it is as strongly unified after the process of revision as it was before. In this, as nowhere else in music, we are admitted to the composer's workshop, and it is most instructive to trace the alterations from the original version, published in 1854,[1] and the later, published in 1891. In the early version, the beautiful flowing subject was disturbed by some rather unnecessary interjections by the violin, which were taken out on revision. The old second subject of the first movement was a mysterious theme of considerable length given out in unison; this became afterwards a finely imagined subject built on an arpeggio figure. The later version of this movement is far closer in its texture than the earlier. In the scherzo the chief alteration is the substitution of a coda of exquisite delicacy and fairy-like charm for the *poco più lento* which formerly wound up the movement with a good deal less point. The slow movement has a more important change, for a subordinate theme in E major has been taken away bodily (not impossibly because it suggested the opening of Schubert's song, *Am Meer*[2]). Its place is taken by a far more

[1] The date, 1859, given in the thematic catalogue, is incorrect. See Kalbeck, i. 163, note 1.

[2] Kalbeck (i. 57) shows that the quotation was intentional.

eloquent and passionate section, and the close of the movement is much shortened. After the first fifty bars or so of the finale, the whole course of the music changes, and almost the only similarity there is between the versions is that both end in B minor, instead of the original major key. The great swinging theme which first appears in D major is peculiar to the new version, and here one feels that the young Brahms of 1854 had not gained the full confidence in the use of his pinions to venture on so bold a flight as carried the man of 1891 to such a perfect end. It may seem like a paradox to speak of unity of style in a work in which so many important alterations were deemed necessary; but the point is that there is not one of the changes which would be detected as such by a person not already familiar with the trio in its earlier version, and that the style of the work as it now stands is at least as homogeneous as that of the original form.

The first sextet for stringed instruments, Op. 18, in B flat, has been well likened to Schubert in its fertility of invention and its wealth of melody. The first movement has no fewer than three of those haunting subjects in slow waltz (or "ländler") time in which Brahms's music is so abundantly rich. The identity of plan at the beginning of the first and last movements has often been noticed, for the violoncello gives out the theme of each and is echoed by the first violin. Originally the first movement began with its present eleventh bar, but Joachim pointed out the great gain in importance which would result if the violoncello started it, and the plan commended itself to the composer so heartily that he employed it again in the finale. The coda, with its use of *pizzicato* in all the instruments but the second violoncello, which holds a pedal F, anticipates the lovely ending of the first movement of the symphony in D. Such things speak so directly and so definitely to the heart that words are wholly inadequate to convey the impression, and the inspired moment can only be compared to some touch of thrilling simplicity in a lyrical poem which makes the reader catch his breath. To analyse such moments is to destroy them, and yet the student must long to find some means by which their exact quality can be conveyed, short of a performance by ideal musicians. In the second movement of the sextet, the first theme of the six variations is given out by the first viola, and each half of it is repeated by a different combination of instruments, the first viola having extended chords as if to maintain its prominence of position. In the first three variations the movement of the figure-work gets more and more rapid, exactly as it does in the variations of Handel and his predecessors, groups of four and six semiquavers being followed by demi-semiquavers. Then comes a quieter major variation, and an exquisite ornamental variation, the first half of which is played on violins and violas alone, the adorned theme being once more given to the first viola. A return is made to the minor mode and the theme in its original form (given out by the first violoncello) for the close of the movement. The energy of the scherzo reminds one not a little of Beethoven, and the trio becomes absolutely uproarious, with a repetition of its uncontrolled behaviour in the coda. The final rondo opens with Haydnesque sedateness, on a theme played by the first violoncello, answered by the three upper strings. As with Mozart, the simple rondo-theme is soon carried to higher issues, and the working-out section contains passages of strenuous dignity particularly at the point where the semiquaver figure is worked against the three-note phrase.

The student of the future, relying exclusively on internal evidence and seeing that the two quartets for piano and strings, Opp. 25 and 26, were published in 1863, the year that Brahms went to live in Vienna, will, of course, conclude that they are the firstfruits of the atmosphere of the Kaiserstadt upon an impressionable nature. But notwithstanding the strongly Hungarian colouring of the first of the two, the beautiful work in G minor, they were both written while Brahms was resident in Germany. But of course Hungarian music was not a sudden revelation to him, for in his earliest days his association with Reményi had made him well acquainted with its characteristics, and its truer nature was revealed to him far more clearly in his close intercourse with Joachim. The sombre colouring of the first movement[1] finds its ideal counterpart in the plaintive grace of the intermezzo, one of those things which are quite peculiar to Brahms. Their fleeting charm and gently elegiac character have never been approached by any composer, ancient or modern. This instance is one of the most beautiful of all. The trio has a suggestion of greater strength, but we willingly fall again under the spell of the yearning weakness, as of a wounded fairy, which seems to be the note of this movement. The lovely andante has not flowed on very far before some arpeggio figures are introduced in the pianoforte part which seem to prophesy one of Brahms's favourite devices, already spoken of in the chapter dealing with his piano music; he seems to attach a mystic significance to this figure, instead of leaving it one of the commonplaces

[1] In the *Joachim Correspondence*, i. 303, is an interesting passage, in which Joachim speaks of the themes of this movement being less pregnant with meaning than is usual with Brahms, but wonders at what he makes out of them. See also p. 306. Madame Schumann's opinion on the two quartets may be compared (Litzmann, iii. 106–7).

of the keyboard, as every one else had done. The feverish animation of the Schubertian passage, which enters at first in C major, is an anticipation of the Hungarian or Gipsy style definitely adopted in the final *Rondo alla Zingarese*, which is justly one of the most popular movements in modern chamber music. The sister quartet, in A major, Op. 26, opens with a passage on the piano which has the delicate poise of a Tanagra figure, its rhythm being as lovely as it is new. The slow movement, *poco adagio*, has a strange colouring, produced, first, by the employment of mutes for the strings while the piano plays *a tre corde*, and, second, by the slight diversity between parts that sound as though in unison.[1] Of course, if played on instruments with exactly the same quality and power of tone, the dissonances which arise from the little incongruity would be ugly; but with the colouring employed, a very beautiful suggestion of hesitancy is given. Schumann

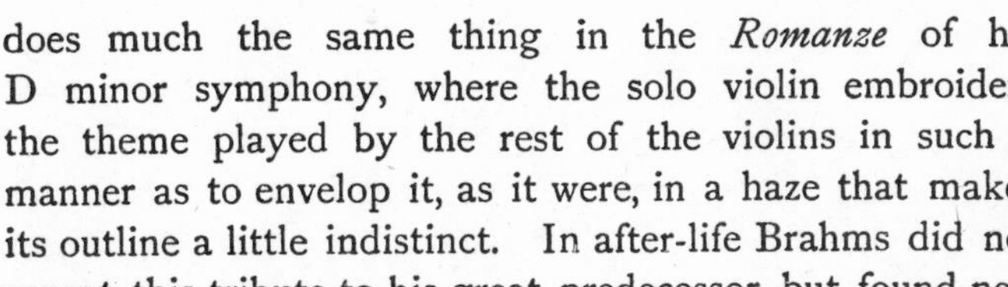

does much the same thing in the *Romanze* of his D minor symphony, where the solo violin embroiders the theme played by the rest of the violins in such a manner as to envelop it, as it were, in a haze that makes its outline a little indistinct. In after-life Brahms did not repeat this tribute to his great predecessor, but found new ways of making his themes sound misty and ethereal. Later on in the movement come in more of the mysterious arpeggios spoken of above; they are played *una corda*, and

[1] See also p. 77.

produce a peculiarly desolate feeling, as of a cold wind blowing over a deserted graveyard. The idea that these arpeggios suggest wind is the only feature which this interpretation has in common with that of Kalbeck, who is reminded by the movement of a lovely spring evening with nightingales in full song. In the scherzo we are in full daylight again, the theme being buoyant and very vigorous; that of the trio, too, with its energetic phrase given out on the piano and repeated in canon by the other instruments, is full of force, and the finale starts with a rhythm caught with difficulty at first even by the sharpest ear. The movement has the animation of some of Schumann's best finales and the ending is unmistakably Schumannesque, with its long dominant pedal and the rapid coda. Many of the early works tell of mastery to be acquired, but these two quartets may well be considered as the earliest things in which that mastery is fully apparent.

The quintet for piano and strings in F minor, Op. 34, went through two transformations before reaching its present state. It was at first a quintet for strings alone, with two violoncellos, but when tried over it was found insufficient in sonority to bear the weight of the important material,[1] and it next became a sonata for two pianofortes. In this guise it was published seven years after its appearance in the ultimate form as the quintet we know. The bold unisons of the opening tell us, as plainly as the first four notes of Beethoven's C minor symphony, that something of great importance is starting, and the prophecy is amply fulfilled, for the work is one of the composer's greatest masterpieces. Mr. Colles has shown how the two parts

[1] See the *Joachim Correspondence*, i. 316 ff., also Litzmann, *Clara Schumann*, iii. 158; she asks Brahms to arrange it for orchestra.

of the first theme are really identical, and in his article on "Sonata" in *Grove's Dictionary* (vol. iv. p. 532), Sir Hubert Parry points out in a very interesting way that a cadence concluding a paragraph is immediately taken up by a

different instrument and embodied as a most significant feature in the accessory subject which follows. It may

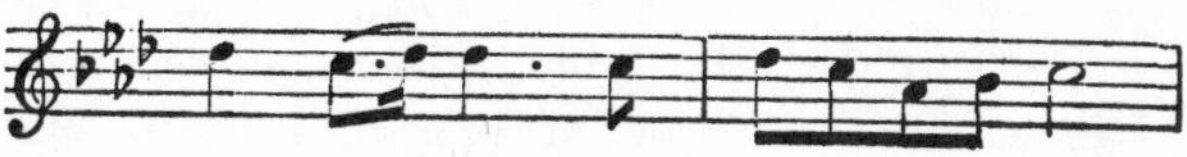

be remarked that the essential part of this theme, the return to the same note after the interruption of a note either immediately above or immediately below it—a kind of enlarged *mordent* or *pralltriller*—is worked through the movement with wonderful effect in the triplet accompaniment and in the more prominent parts at the same time. The pure lyricism of the *andante un poco adagio* is of a rare beauty which even Brahms seldom surpassed, and the arrangement of its delivery by the various instruments is so varied and so delightful to the ear that there is no fear of the sweetness of the theme becoming too cloying. The exquisite little coda is a worthy ending to the movement. The scherzo, in which the pulsating rhythm is set at first by the violoncello on reiterated C's played *pizzicato*, has an irresistible swing, and the varying paces of a horse are suggested in the alternation of $\frac{2}{4}$ with $\frac{6}{8}$ time, though the beats of the bars never alter. The trio keeps up the same motion, and the abrupt ending of the section with a cadence that falls upon the keynote from the semitone above is not its least original feature. The introduction to the finale is another tribute to Schumann's favourite way of opening his last movements; it is slow and mysterious, and those who study it minutely will find that the germ of it is contained in the rising phrase of two notes, generally a semitone, sometimes a whole tone, which phrase eventually generates the strenuous *allegro non troppo.* The coda in $\frac{6}{8}$ time recalls the figure of the scherzo, and its pace becomes apparently uncontrollable before the close of the whole.

The second sextet for strings, Op. 36, in G, will always divide with the first the preferences of musicians; it is quite impossible to say that one is beyond question superior to the other, although the second has the greater maturity which we should expect. Its first *allegro* starts on a groundwork of a wavering tonic pedal sustained on the first viola, and the main theme alternates very boldly between the keys of G and E flat. Both these elements combine to make the working out of the movement one of the most interesting in existence, even without the help of the attractive second subject—a suave melody in which, as in the first theme, Brahms's fondness for tunes built on the successive notes of a chord shows itself. The scherzo is worked with masterly skill, but it is a little overshadowed by the irresistible merriment and spontaneity of the *presto giocoso*, the delivery of which by Joachim and his colleagues can never be forgotten by those who heard it, so full was it of the suggestion of perennial youth. The slow movement consists of five variations and a coda on a soaring theme (nearly allied to the first theme of the opening movement), given out by the first violin, supported by the second violin and first viola in a cross-rhythm of four quavers against six. The third variation is in vigorous imitation and may be compared with the finale of the violoncello sonata, Op. 38; the fifth, a flowing *adagio*, is in the major, and the coda gathers up the characteristics of the theme. The finale opens with a quasi-tremolando passage on the chord of the supertonic, so that our sense of key-relationship is agreeably surprised. The *tranquillo* theme is a fine contrast to the first, and the working out of the movement is most exciting.[1]

Op. 38, the first sonata for piano and violoncello, in E minor, opens with so straightforward and obvious a theme in the lower notes of the stringed instrument that the entry of the second subject, a swaying, harmonic figure, is doubly welcome, and a subordinate theme to this latter, occurring just before the double-bar, is beautiful in itself and bears an important part in the development of the movement. The *allegretto quasi menuetto* has a gait of remarkable grace, and its main theme is ushered in by a little cadential figure, which contains the germ not only of much of the minuet, but of the theme of the trio; this stands in the distant key of F sharp minor, the minuet being in A minor. The *allegro* has a powerful fugal opening, the suggestion for which may possibly be found in the third variation of the slow movement of the G major sextet. There are stretti, episodes, and other peculiarities of fugal writing, and the section is of unsurpassable brilliance and importance.

Op. 40, the well-known trio for piano, violin, and horn, is a lasting disproof of the charge that Brahms cared nothing for effects of tone-colour. His use of the

[1] See Litzmann's *Clara Schumann*, iii. 171.

horn in combination with the other instruments is so characteristic and so admirably skilful that when the place of that instrument is taken by violoncello or viola much is inevitably lost. (The latter instrument is the more effective of the two permitted substitutes.) The first and second subjects of the opening movement are of infinite grace and eloquence, the scherzo has some suggestion of the hunting scenes with which the tone of horns is most commonly associated, and the *adagio mesto* is pregnant with poetical meaning; at one point, not far from the end, the violin has a couple of bars in F major, from which would seem to be derived the joyous theme of the finale in which the horn's favourite kind of passage is conspicuous. By its moderate length, its genial character, and the beauty of its colouring, this trio is one of the most popular of Brahms's works.

In the central period of Brahms's work, after the *Requiem* and near the other great choral works and the first *Liebeslieder*, his only contribution to concerted chamber music was the pair of string quartets published in 1873 as Op. 51. He was wise, no doubt, to leave quartet-writing until he had proved himself in the other great branches of music; for of them all, the quartet is surely the greatest test of a composer's real power. So narrow are the limits imposed, that nothing but real fine workmanship through and through will lead to success; yet the means are sufficient to express deep and poetical thoughts, and there is no feeling that a difficult problem has been solved, as there is in a composition for three stringed instruments. The two quartets were by no means the composer's first attempts in that form; he told a friend[1] that he had written

[1] Kalbeck, ii. 429.

as many as twenty string-quartets before achieving one that seemed to him good enough to publish. The first of the two, in C minor, suggests that, as Brahms had been so fully engaged in the composition of things which were definitely meant for the public at large, he willingly turned to a style of music which could appeal only to the few who care to probe the depths of a great man's thought. The opening allegro is not at all easy to follow or to grasp even with every advantage of performance and previous knowledge of the score. As Mr. Colles says, "Even the distinction of first and second subject is difficult, so completely does each phrase seem to grow out of the last." It remains a masterly piece of musical development, and if the romance in A flat is almost too "intimate" for most people, the intermezzo in F minor has a winning charm, and its trio in F major is entrancing in its perfect simplicity and naïve grace. At its commencement a beautiful undulating effect is produced by the second violin reiterating the note A on the open string and a stopped string alternately. The severity of the first movement is continued in the finale, and both movements are for the student rather than for the public. It is all the more curious on this account that here, of all places, Herr Kalbeck should have discovered two unconscious quotations from the Wagnerian trilogy, the "Erda-theme" at the opening of the first movement and the "Walhall-theme" at the opening of the second.[1] The latter is of far slighter extent than the former, but it is an odd coincidence that both should come from the same quarter and be embodied in surroundings where the average Wagnerian would be most unlikely to look for them. The second quartet in A

[1] Kalbeck, ii. 451.

minor is far more intelligible to ordinary hearers, and it contains in its first notes the virtual dedication to Joachim, although the two quartets are dedicated ostensibly to Dr. Billroth. The notes "F, A, E," standing for "Frei, aber einsam," represent the motto which stood with Joachim for the ideal of his career. The quartets were brought out during a short period of estrangement between Joachim and Brahms, and the treatment of Joachim's artistic motto in this way had its share in bringing about a reconciliation.[1] The opening notes, A, F, A, are said by the author to stand for a musical motto of Brahms himself, so that the union of the two phrases had a special personal meaning.[2] They appear with a marked distinctness at the opening in the first violin part, and contain the germ of much that is to follow. The second subject is of the most gracious beauty, and a subordinate theme in which triplets of crotchets are prominent helps to carry on the interest of the movement. The *andante moderato* is deeply poetical, but in rather a sombre mood, and the *quasi minuetto* breaks in upon it with great charm. The alternation of this movement with an *allegretto vivace* in A major is one of the characteristic things in the work, and foreshadows the similar device in the violin sonata, Op. 100. The finale is a remarkable achievement in the way of transformation of the main theme, which appears in no fewer than eight different shapes in its course, ending with a version in slow chords, *pianissimo*, leading to a *più vivace*, which ends the work in brilliant style.

After a considerable space of time, occupied by the *Liebeslieder* and various large choral works, a third

[1] See Kalbeck, ii. 443 ff. [2] But see note on p. 90.

quartet for piano and strings made its appearance as Op. 60. It is in C minor, and is far less often played than the two sister quartets for the same combination. It is not surprising that it should be so, for it is one of the least easy to grasp of all the master's works, although when it is known it is deeply loved. There is a curious story associated with its first movement, for in the summer of 1868 the composer showed it (it had been written as early as 1855) to Hermann Deiters, and prepared him to listen to it with these words: "Now, think of a man who is just going to shoot himself, because there is nothing else left for him to do." Kalbeck[1] says that Brahms spoke with such gravity as to leave the impression on Deiters's mind that he himself had passed through some such experience; but we may surely indulge the hope that the mood was merely imaginary, and that a written sentence to Dr. Billroth points the way to the proper comprehension of the emotional purport of the movement. He says, "It is an illustration of the last chapter about the man in the blue coat and yellow waistcoat." These words are enough to convey to any cultivated German the description of the dead Werther in Goethe's romance. Whether any admirers of Brahms are likely to enjoy the quartet more because they think of Werther, I do not know. To return to comfortable matters of fact, Mr. Colles points out that the second section of the first movement is a little set of variations on the theme first played by the piano, which are still further added to in the reprise. The scherzo takes us back to the style of the "horn trio," and the slow movement, with its richly melodious subject given out at first by the

[1] i. 241.

violoncello, is Brahms of the purest kind. The finale, with a figure in the manner of a *moto perpetuo*, is very effective.[1]

The third quartet for strings alone, Op. 67, in B flat, is the last of the chamber compositions in which any trace is to be found of the austerity of style with which it was formerly the fashion to reproach the composer. The unceasing movement of the quavers in $\frac{6}{8}$ time is relieved very happily by short sections in $\frac{2}{4}$ time, which have a most humorous effect. The theme of the andante, delivered by the first violin, has a kind of royal serenity and ease about it which foreshadows the style of much of the composer's later works; the *agitato* that comes after it is most plaintive, and the subject is given out by the unmuted viola, the other three being played *con sordino*. The *poco allegretto con variazioni* is one of the loveliest themes in existence, absolutely simple in design and deliciously fresh in invention. Six variations pass, changing keys and figures, and after the sixth, in G flat, we are surprised by a sudden return, not only to the original key of B flat, but to the theme of the first movement, which is made to do duty as a variation, while for the close the theme of the variations and this initial subject of the whole work are joined in with exquisite effect. "Austerity" is in truth not the right word to apply to such a tenderly eloquent work as this quartet; perhaps "intimacy" will better express the quality which prevents it from being a very general favourite. Some strange analytical remarks upon it may be read in Kalbeck,[2] as, for example, that the opening

[1] For Joachim's interesting criticism, see the *Correspondence* with him, i. 124–7.

[2] ii. 455 ff.

theme of the first movement has a similarity to that of a trumpery old piano piece, which was fashionable (and no doubt composed) long after this quartet was published, under the name *Gavotte de Louis XIII.* The habit of hunting for reminiscences is apt to get quite irrepressible, and this instance may serve as a warning not to attach too much importance to other examples which Kalbeck cites.

The sonata for piano and violin in G, Op. 78, did not appear until after the symphonies Nos. 1 and 2 were published, and it would almost seem as if in these and the violin concerto a gentler, more appealing manner of expression followed from the use of the orchestra, for from this point onwards almost everything belongs to the class of music that is appreciable at once by the educated hearer, and after a short acquaintance by the less accomplished. The sonata brought Brahms more friends than perhaps any other of his compositions, partly due, no doubt, to the zeal with which Joachim spread its beauty through Europe. Other violinists were not slow in taking up the piece, and it has never lost its hold in the thirty years since it appeared. Its lovely tenderness of expression all through, the unity of its style, and the deftness with which the two instruments are treated, all combine to make it widely beloved. The initial phrase of the first movement, with the three repeated notes, the first in dotted rhythm, foreshadows the theme of the finale, which is identical with the subject of the two songs in Op. 59 (published in 1873), *Regenlied* and *Nachklang*, and the slow movement which comes between the movements, and which interrupts the course of the last movement, makes an irresistible appeal to all who love musical beauty.

Three years after this appeared two more concerted pieces, the trio for piano and strings in C major, Op. 87, and the string quintet, Op. 88. If both these works have been practically overshadowed by Op. 101 and Op. 111 respectively, it is pretty certain that as time goes on their beauties will be more and more widely appreciated, even though their younger sisters may still be preferred by most players and listeners. The trio, starting with a broad unisonous phrase, has, in its *allegro*, one of those lovely, yearning second subjects that are peculiar to Brahms; the slow movement, in A minor, is a set of five variations on a theme of a character nearly allied to what is known as the Hungarian type of folk-tune. The scherzo is genuine fairy-music, beginning with a phrase of gossamer texture into which there breaks, at the trio, a suggestion of fairy horns and signals. The finale has something almost grotesque in its rather stolid figure of accompaniment, which makes of course a perfect contrast to what has just been heard. The quintet in F, Op. 88, begins with a splendid example of concise development on a strongly rhythmical subject, and its second movement presents us with a strange new feature, for it is interrupted twice over, the first time by a section of pastoral simplicity in A, $\frac{6}{8}$, and afterwards by a presto in the same key, $\frac{4}{4}$, the main theme returning at first in C sharp major, and at last in A major, after each contrasting episode. It is of such beautiful breadth and suavity that the interruptions might well be resented, if they were less beautiful than they are. The finale starts fugally, and the strict style is maintained for some time, with free use of episodical matter; a coda, *presto*, winds up the work very satisfactorily.[1]

[1] See Frau von Herzogenberg's remarks on it in the *Correspondence* with her, i. 191 ff.; trans., 167 ff.

Not until after the fourth symphony did the next piece of instrumental ensemble see the light. Op. 99, the sonata for piano and violoncello in F, was published in 1887; it opens in a mood of wild energy such as is not frequent in Brahms's later works; the unrest is increased by the unusually distant key chosen for the slow movement, for F sharp major is not a common successor to F major, though it is easily explained by reference to the key of D flat, to which the main key is the mediant or third of the scale, and F sharp the subdominant key (by enharmonic change). The slow movement is of remarkable sonority, and bears traces of having been intended for the late Professor Hausmann's dignified and virile style of playing. The *allegro passionato* in F minor and the solidly built finale are worthy of the master, even if the work as a whole numbers fewer friends than some of his other compositions. Of these, there is none more engaging than Op. 100, the sonata for piano and violin in A major, which ever since its first appearance in 1887 has been a serious rival to the first sonata. The superficial likeness in its first theme to the "Preislied" of *Die Meistersinger* was made the most of twenty years ago, but people have by this time found that the similarity goes no further than the first three notes. The *andante tranquillo* is as lovely as a song, and the *vivace*, which alternates with it after a fashion we have traced in one or two instances lately spoken of, lends itself admirably to the purpose, becoming more and more rapid with each repetition. The finale has certain points in common with the song *Auf dem Kirchhofe* from Op. 105, and reference may be made here to a letter in the *Herzogenberg Correspondence*, vol. ii. p. 140 (p. 298 of the English translation). From that it is clear that the song was really written first, though published two years after the sonata.

Op. 101 is the splendid trio for piano and strings in C minor, a work distinguished in the highest degree, both for invention and treatment. No theme was ever more energetic than its opening, none more broadly flowing than its second subject, nor anything more concise and to the point than its development. The *presto non assai* is one of those plaintive "April" movements which are Brahms's speciality; the pianoforte chords and the *pizzicato* passages which distinguish the middle section may be held to be æsthetically connected with the mysterious use of arpeggios, of which we have so many examples. The *andante grazioso* begins with a dialogue, the two stringed instruments giving out the first phrase and the piano repeating them with amplified harmonies. The theme itself is in a rhythm expressed as a bar of $\frac{3}{4}$ time, followed by two bars of $\frac{2}{4}$ time; of course this is actually a long bar of seven crotchets, with subordinate accents on the fourth and sixth beats. But no one would guess that there was anything out of the way in rhythm, so suave and serene is the movement of the theme, and so broad and calm its flow. A short alternative section in what the pundits would call "compound quintuple time" (*i.e.*, alternate bars of $\frac{9}{8}$ and $\frac{6}{8}$ time) comes in by way of relief, but, in spite of the verbal intricacies in which alone an accurate idea of the music can be given apart from actual performance, the whole movement is one of the most spontaneous in Brahms's works. The vigour of the first movement returns in the last, in the course of which the reappearance of the main theme in the tonic major is like a gleam of sunshine on a cloudy day.

In 1889, two years after this, came the third of the violin sonatas, Op. 108 in D minor, a work of stronger texture but no less charm than the other two violin sonatas. One of its peculiarities is the *sforzando* note in an unexpected part of the bar in the second subject of the first movement, a passage to which very few players, by the way, know how to give the exact value, some of them avoiding the emphasis altogether, and some overdoing it. The effect is at its best if the increase of force be only comparatively slight, but if the smallest imaginable break be made after it, in fact if more attention be paid to the staccato mark than to the *sf.* The famous dominant pedal point which occurs in this movement, lasting for forty-six bars, carries us back to the pedal fugue in the *Requiem*, and in its way is as fine as that. The slow movement is of rare directness and simplicity of structure, though it deals with great emotional passion. The movement labelled *Un poco presto e con sentimento* is, of all the elfin movements of Brahms, the most fairy-like, for its sadness is not human, like that of the preceding movement, and its exquisite beauty must appeal to every one who is not deaf to imaginative poetry. The passage in which the pianoforte part suggests, rather than plays, a descending scale, quite at the end, is ravishingly beautiful. The swing of the last movement is irresistible, and the suave theme which relieves it reminds us of the third theme in the last movement of the piano sonata, Op. 5, by its serenity and breadth.[1]

The string quintet, Op. 111, which appeared in 1891, opens with a passage concerning which there is a good deal in the letters.[2] There was a feeling that no one but Hausmann could possibly make the opening theme on the violon-

[1] On the difficult passage ot syncopation in the finale, p. 28, see the *Herzogenberg Correspondence*, vol. ii. p. 215 ff.; trans., 365 ff.

[2] See the *Herzogenberg Correspondence*, ii. 245–6; trans., 392; and the *Joachim Correspondence*, ii. 239–42.

cello tell against the other strings if they were allowed to play *forte* with the sonorous *tremolando* set down for them. It was found advisable to let them play *mezzo-forte* with ordinary violoncellists, though the *forte* remains in the printed copies. The wonderful swing of the opening theme is finely contrasted with the half-hesitating gait of the two subordinate subjects, the first given out by the first viola, the other by the second violin. The first viola, throughout the work, has an unusually large share of the "leading" to do. The adagio in D minor is in its hands, and near the end there is a cadenza for the same instrument. The *poco allegretto* has a less important part for the first viola until we get to the trio, where it leads again. At the close of the main section, before the trio, and again before the coda in which the trio-theme is resumed, there is a curious instance of unconscious plagiarism, for in the last chorus of Bach's *St. Matthew Passion*, the two orchestras answer one another with this phrase—

while in Brahms's quintet, the following two bars—

have so exactly the same colouring that the reminder is inevitable. Of course no kind of imputation is suggested on the later master, but it is so rare to find him departing, even by four notes, from absolute originality of idea, that the case is worth pointing out.

The trio begins with a phrase that seems to have come straight from some very simple folk-song; it is halved, so to speak, between the viola and the first violin, and at the coda, when it reappears, the two half-phrases are presented, first by the two violins in inverted form, and next by the two violas the right way up. The first viola opens the finale with a busy theme, the working-out of which is especially interesting; a unisonous run for all the instruments leads to a coda of unmistakably Hungarian colour.

Next on the list, and closing the master's productions in this class, come four works, the composition of which was beyond question suggested to Brahms by the admirable clarinet-playing of Professor Mühlfeld, the distinguished member of the Meiningen Orchestra, whose exquisite art was also a special feature of the early performances of *Parsifal* at Bayreuth. The trio, Op. 114, in A minor, is for piano, clarinet (or viola), and violoncello; the first movement shows fine development of two well-contrasted subjects, and its crossing scale-passages are made use of at the close very effectively. The theme of the *adagio* is no distant relation of the second subject of the allegro, and the movement is genuinely expressive; the subject of the *andantino grazioso* has been quoted in Chapter III, and not all its lovely development can quite atone for a want of distinction, of which it is the only instance in Brahms's music. The finale is in a mixture of $\frac{2}{4}$ and $\frac{6}{8}$ time, such as Brahms always loved, but the whole trio has suffered by the simultaneous publication of one of the most masterly and the loveliest of all the master's works, the quintet for clarinet and strings in B minor, Op. 115. Of the first movement, Mr. Colles well says: "The first movement seems to contain all things, the best of his life's experience, surpassing beauty, infinite tenderness, with here and there a gleam of that rugged strength which characterised all his art." From the opening phrase in thirds on the two violins, we feel enchanted by the twisting sextolets of semiquavers, and the second subject, by way of breaking through the usual convention, is of a more vigorous strain than the first. The *adagio* is one of the most poetical things in the whole of music; its melody is long-drawn, and above an accompaniment full of cross-rhythms, played on the muted strings, the clarinet notes soar with a beauty that is almost unearthly. The rhapsodical middle section is obviously designed with particular reference to the clarinet and its facility in rapid passages, and at the close of the movement there is a dialogue between the first violin and the clarinet which cannot be forgotten by any who had the happiness of hearing the quintet interpreted with Joachim and Mühlfeld in these parts. The clarinettist seemed to express, in the *pianissimo* phrase, the inmost secrets of the human heart in a mood of passionate rapture; one thought, as he played, that the smallest touch more must end in exaggeration; yet when Joachim took up the phrase he put even more into it than Mühlfeld had done, and yet kept it entirely within the picture and within the bounds of truest art. The *andantino*, starting with a very square-cut theme, contains a very interesting instance of the transformation of material, such as is found in the second symphony; for the *presto non assai*, though not textually the same, is very nearly allied to it. The variations, five in number, which form the finale, are built on a lovely theme, in which each phrase is echoed rather sadly by the clarinet, after being given out by the strings. The first variation opens with the violoncello alone, and here Signor Piatti, who first played the work in England, used to make a great impression by his delicious phrasing. At the third variation we begin to be let into the secret of what is to come, for the echoing phrase, from the opening of the movement, has a little twist given to it which henceforth is never quite out of sight until, for the coda to the whole work, the opening theme of the first movement is heard once more. From beginning to end, the quintet is so lovely that all musicians must be thankful that Professor Mühlfeld lived to inspire it, although, as Mr. Colles says: "Had Brahms never heard the great clarinettist, that music must have been expressed somehow." No doubt; but the mode of expression must have been different, and it is impossible to conceive any change that could have improved it.

It remains only to speak of the two sonatas for pianoforte and clarinet, which were published together, in 1895, as Op. 120. The first, in F minor, has a first movement which is not easy either to play or to comprehend; its most attractive moment is the sostenuto at the close, where the two instruments have beautifully characteristic passages. The *andante* breathes the calm, melancholy atmosphere of the quintet that has just been described; and the *allegretto* has a winsome grace like some lovely and individual dance movement. The finale always seems to promise a strictly contrapuntal treatment of the repeated minims at the opening, but though these are very prominent rhythmically through the movement, the working-out proceeds along more usual lines. The second sonata will always be the favourite both with musicians and with the public, for its tender appeal is irresistible, and its themes are one and all of that attractive kind which distinguished the last period of Brahms's work. The style of the opening *allegro amabile* carries us back to the first violin sonata, not in its thematic material, but by its general mood. The *allegro appassionato*, which comes next, seems almost too important in structure for its place, for though it conforms to the type of scherzo with trio, the scherzo theme is so rich in musical suggestion that one expects it to be more fully developed than it can be in the space. The *sostenuto*, too, belongs to the broadest things that Brahms was ever inspired to write. A free set of variations comes as the last movement. The third variation reminds us a little of the second intermezzo from Op. 117, but the figure is divided between the two instruments. The allegro variation, which immediately precedes the coda, is in the master's most vigorous vein, and the old use of pianoforte arpeggios with a sense of menace comes to light just once more before the end of the sonata. After this Brahms wrote no more for instruments in combination.

BRAHMS CONDUCTING

FROM A DRAWING BY PROF. W. VON BECKERATH

CHAPTER VI

THE ORCHESTRAL WORKS

BRAHMS'S first essay in orchestral writing immediately preceded his first attempt to write for chorus; it was in 1860 that his Op. 11 appeared, in a lithographed score. It is a serenade for full orchestra (with four horns and no trombones), and is in the key of D major. It is curious to see how the unusual vehicle seems at first to hamper the freedom of his expression; it is not easy to realize that after the first trio, the Schumann variations, and the *Balladen*, a man who had acquired, in piano solo music and in concerted chamber music, so much certainty of utterance, should feel oppressed by the orchestra, as he seems to have done. Mr. Colles has well said: "This serenade bows in turn to each classical predecessor, Haydn, Schubert, and the early manner of Beethoven, and accepts unhesitatingly each convention of orchestration that they used." The second subject of the first allegro is the earliest example in the work of a manner which may be called Brahms's own, and while the first scherzo is charming and individual, the slow movement is certainly open to the charge often levelled unjustly against the whole of Brahms's orchestral music, that it is too thickly scored. The two minuets are the most successful part of the work; the first is scored for first flute, first and second clarinets, first bassoon and violoncello, while, in the second, the two clarinets take part with the violas and violoncellos. There is a lovely coda in which the viola has a descending passage between the held notes of the flute and violoncello. The second scherzo, for all its indebtedness to Beethoven, and particularly to the ninth symphony, has some individuality, and the final rondo, with its schoolboy humour, must always be effective.

As a matter of fact, the first pianoforte concerto, Op. 15, in D minor, was written before the first serenade,[1] and actually made its appearance in public before that work; but it seems more convenient to adhere to the order of opus-numbers in analysing the compositions. The story of the unfavourable reception accorded to the concerto has been told elsewhere (see pp. 10, 11). Brahms took his failure like a man, and, so far from disheartening him, it strung him to new efforts, and the disappointment bore good fruit. But, looked at from the point of view of his later music, the first piano concerto seems to have been most unfairly judged by the Leipzig public; at all events, their verdict has been emphatically set aside by the world in general, with whom the concerto has of late years taken its place among the more frequently performed of the master's works with orchestra. It is easy to see wherein lay the cause of the animosity it aroused. The opening, which now strikes the hearer as a splendid demonstration of vigour, must have offended the pundits with its chord

[1] It existed in the form of a sonata for two pianos as early as 1854 (see the *Joachim Correspondence*, i. 28, 52). It was next turned into a symphony, but it is not clear that it was finished in that form. As a concerto, its first movement was being written out at the end of 1856 (see Litzmann's *Clara Schumann*, iii. 17). It was long before it satisfied the composer, and his fine expressions of dissatisfaction may be read in Litzmann, *op. cit.*, iii. 25.

of the sixth on the tonic, and although the long exposition of the material of the movement which precedes the entry of the solo instrument was quite in accord with conservative tradition, yet the introduction of apparently new material when the piano comes in, and the admittedly "thick" style of orchestration in the preludial section, may well have been a stumbling-block to the hearers of the first performance. It is curious that the second subject is not fully discussed with the rest of the material in the first orchestral passage, but it is all the more effective for being left to the piano to deliver; it is of great beauty, and its continuation, with a swaying figure that afterwards becomes of great prominence, should, one thinks, have won all hearts and finally conquered when it is brought in on the horn. It is unlike Brahms's later habit to put the slow movement into the same rhythm as the first; but at its first conception the slow movement was altogether different, containing the germs of what afterwards became the striking funeral march movement in triple time in the *Requiem*. In spite of the identity of rhythmic shape between the two movements as they now stand, there is so marked a difference of character between the suave adagio and the vigorous opening movement that no lack of contrast is felt. The first movement has been held—and as the information came from Joachim there is every reason to believe it—to have been inspired by the tragedy of Schumann's attempt at suicide, and the second, in the autograph score formerly in the possession of Joachim, bears the inscription "Benedictus qui venit in nomine domini," which Kalbeck interprets as another allusion to Schumann, whom Brahms sometimes addressed as "Mynheer Domine." As originally conceived the work showed yet another remarkable variation from its present shape, for the finale which was first written to it was no less genial an inspiration than the last movement of the symphony in C minor. It really seems a little hard on the concerto that it should once have possessed two of the most individual movements in the whole of the master's work, and had to sacrifice them, even though their later form is no doubt far more amply and maturely developed than the earlier. The present rondo of the concerto is vigorous and buoyant, and the cadenza which leads so fantastically into the fine resumption of the main theme in the tonic major is most effective.

The next work for orchestra, Op. 16, is a second serenade, in A major, for small orchestra, consisting of two flutes, two oboes, two clarinets, two bassoons, two horns, violas, violoncellos, and double-basses. The experiment of dispensing with the violins was tried again in the opening chorus of the *Requiem* (see p. 203). Here it seems to have been in some sort adopted as an exercise in scoring (a letter from Joachim to Madame Schumann, printed in Litzmann, iii. 46, shows that Brahms was still giving much thought to various ways of scoring it), or possibly the composer may have felt that his use of the violins in the other serenade was too constant, and have denied himself their employment altogether for the purpose of getting ease and certainty in writing for the rest of the orchestra. The serenade is not of great importance for the general musical public, though it will always be beloved by those who discern in it the promise of what was to come in the author's maturer works. In the light of these, the first movement is seen to have very interesting developments, and the whole has remarkable charm, spontaneity, and grace. The scherzo in C major has a suggestion of those crossing rhythms which are the most obvious of Brahms's characteristics, and the trio, given out by the clarinets and bassoons in unison, carries on a suave and broad theme above the persistent rhythm of the scherzo. The adagio is no doubt the most beautiful movement, striking a note of deeper emotion than any of the others, and containing a lovely passage in the middle for the wind instruments alone. The *Quasi Menuetto* has a halting rhythm of exceedingly characteristic daintiness, and the final rondo is built on a theme which even on paper tells one who was the author. It is in some way analogous in pattern to the opening movement of the "horn trio." The first edition of the second serenade appeared in 1860, but the state in which it is best known dates from 1875, when the composer had revised it in some details. It is minutely analysed in Kalbeck, i. 381–5.

After it, although of course the orchestra was used in the *Requiem*, the *Schicksalslied*, *Rinaldo*, and other vocal works, Brahms did not write for orchestra alone until Op. 56*a*, the variations on a theme of Haydn which had appeared in 1873 as a duet for two pianos, the orchestral form not being published until 1874. It occurs in one of Haydn's MS. "divertimenti" for brass instruments, and the tune is there headed "Chorale St. Antoni" (*sic*). Whether it is Haydn's in the beginning or not is quite unknown, but no one has yet traced it to an older source. The theme is given out almost exactly as it is in Haydn, and a contrafagotto is very prominent in the opening. Not till the first variation do the violins come in; in a beautiful contrapuntal passage two quavers are played against three, and in all the likeness to the theme is often a little difficult to trace at a first hearing. In the second variation a persistent pizzicato bass supports the movement of the clarinet and bassoon; in the third the oboe and bassoon have a sinuous figure above a striking unison passage for violins and violoncellos. The unisonous treatment of the oboe and the horn in the fourth variation is one of the very few points where the scoring is not entirely felicitous. In variation five the wind instruments, with a piccolo added to the score, keep up a busy chattering over a kind of pedal-passage in the strings. No. 6 brings out the characteristics of the horn with splendid effect, and No. 7, in which the delicious falling theme is played on the flute and viola in octaves, is perhaps the most popular passage of the whole work. In No. 8 the piccolo is used with singularly haunting effect among the gloomy surroundings of the muted strings. The serene opening of the finale on the bass of the theme tells us of what is to come, as surely as Beethoven tells us that matters of great moment are in his mind at the beginning of the last movement of the *Eroica* symphony. The increasing elaboration of the workmanship up to the climax where first the wind instruments and then the strings have a rushing scale, is among the most powerful of musical impressions of any date, and while all the variations are a delight to the ear, whether on the orchestra or on the pianos, yet the best is kept till the last, and the learning displayed is only used to enable the master to make the effect he wants upon his hearers. Even the most hide-bound of critics can hardly maintain after hearing this work that Brahms had no feeling for orchestral colour. As well might he be denied the skill of counterpoint, which is the most obvious feature of the finale. A fanciful analysis of the variations may be read in Kalbeck, ii. 463 ff.; the author attempts to read into the work a musical picture of the temptation of St. Anthony!

In 1877 appeared the master's first actual symphony, Op. 68, in C minor. As a matter of course so important a work by an author so vehemently discussed was sure to provoke his professed enemies to a manifestation of disapproval, and his friends to expressions of perhaps extreme partiality. On the one side it was pointed out that the orchestration, particularly in the first movement, was thick and "muddy," that the themes of the opening were of so slight a quality as hardly to bear the weight of development put upon them, and that the first hearing of the work failed to charm the casual hearer by any special point of loveliness at once irresistible. The fact that the finale theme is identical in general rhythmic shape with that of the finale of Beethoven's ninth symphony was not forgotten by the opponents of Brahms, who have indeed never ceased, in all the years that have elapsed since the symphony was written, from hinting at plagiarism in this respect. It is a point to which reference must be made later; those who wish to read the opinions of the various German critics may consult Miss May's *Life*, vol. ii. chap. xviii. In regard to the thickness of the orchestration, an accusation for which there is indeed some ground, the case is almost a parallel to certain poems of Browning; the thoughts are so weighty, the reasoning, as it may be called, so close, that the ordinary means of expression are inadequate to convey the whole of what is in the creator's mind, and a feeling of strain is undoubtedly caused at certain moments. But to try to rescore such a movement as this with the sacrifice of none of its meaning, is as hopeless a task as to rewrite *Sordello* in sentences that a child should understand. As has been said before, there can be no doubt that the shortcomings in scoring in this and some other movements of Brahms arise from his temporary indifference to, not from any inability to handle, orchestral colour. The introductory portion is no doubt severe in mood, and its simultaneous exposition of two themes, one ascending, the other descending, makes it difficult to grasp. To those who know the whole symphony, it comes like the promise of a rare joy that reaches its fulfilment in the final allegro. There is, even at a first hearing, a wonderful rhythmic swing about the whole movement, and its development from germs that at first seemed of very slight quality shows again the mastery of the composer, even if he has chosen to create this development at the cost of some passages that might have tickled the ears of the audience. On the question of a poetical suggestion from *Manfred*, Kalbeck's *Life*, i. 243 ff. may be consulted. The slow movement, *andante sostenuto*, has plenty of orchestral effect, and its lyrical form might, one would think, have propitiated even those who were most hostile to the composer. There occurs in it a short passage which, without any definite literary or poetical suggestion from outside, comes as near as anything in music to the place where tones have all the eloquence and definiteness of words. The seven bars given out first by the oboe, and later on by a violin solo as well, have all the satisfaction of a perfect syllogism, all the beauty of the highest poetry, and in listening to them as they come in their place in the movement, one actually seems to take in and apprehend some idea that transcends words and music alike. The impression fades almost as soon as it is created, like the remembrance of a dream at the moment of waking; but one can recall its presence, and that presence is called up each time the work is heard. At the point where it seems to approach its natural ending, the instrument that has given out the phrase stops, and a kind of warning phrase is uttered pianissimo, at first by bassoon, horns, and strings, and subsequently by flute, clarinets, and bassoons, as if the complete utterance of the whole would have transgressed some spiritual law, and let humanity into some divine secret. The light-hearted *poco allegretto* which stands in the place of a scherzo gives the most perfect relief between the *andante* and the solemn introduction to the finale. There is, notwithstanding, a moment in the alternative section which gives a touch of mystery that is in keeping with the work as a whole. The *adagio* which prefaces the finale begins with a descending phrase in the wind recalling the opening of the symphony; against this is now played in the violin parts a theme which eventually becomes the joyous theme of the *allegro*. At the fifth complete bar there begins a mysterious passage of pizzicato quavers, which are gradually quickened[1] to a most exciting point, where a drum roll ushers in a series of notes on the horn marked "*f sempre e passionato*" supported by the strings, muted and *tremolando*. A correlative theme of hymn-like squareness, in which the trombones make their first prominent appearance in the work, brings back the horn-phrase, imitated by various other wind instruments, like a signal passing from one watcher to another before the sunrise. On the occasion when the symphony was played for the first time in England, at Cambridge on 8 March,

[1] Herr Arthur Nikisch, in order to enhance the effect of this quickening, starts these quavers so slowly that they are almost identical in length with the crotchets that have preceded them. Whether it is permissible to upset the whole balance of the section for such an object may be doubted, especially when such conductors as Joachim, Richter, and Steinbach, who had the master's own traditions, give no support to this reading. Each of these great conductors was accustomed to make certain *rallentandos* at various points of the first movement, and as no written *rallentando* occurs there, the probability is that Brahms at different times of his life approved of the different readings, and at all events that he did not actively disapprove of any.

1877, the audience in the Guildhall heard the horn-phrase answered, as it seemed, by the chimes of St. Mary's Church, close at hand, for the notes of the horn-phrase are virtually identical with those of the last part of the "Cambridge Quarters." This of course has nothing to do with the symphony itself, and the coincidence probably lessened the emotional effect of the introduction, which reaches its climax at the entry of the allegro movement. There is no doubt, as Miss May has said, "that every one who listens to Brahms's first symphony thinks immediately, on the entrance of the final allegro, of Beethoven's ninth." But she adds, very truly, "The association passes with the conclusion of the subject; Brahms's movement develops on its own lines, which do not resemble those of Beethoven." The curious thing is that in the two themes there is little, if any, resemblance in the melodic curve or in the sequence of notes; both are strongly and exclusively diatonic in movement and in harmony, and the younger theme, equally with the older, belongs to the most precious things in the treasury of music. Shortly before the end of the movement, the horn-phrase is again heard, most impressively, and is worked up together with the flowing second subject and other things into a brilliant climax.

Only a year after the first symphony was published the second, in D, Op. 73. Of the four, this work is far more often heard than the others, and it is not surprising that it should be so, for it is not only scored all through with more regard to popular effect, but its material is of such comparatively slight quality that it can be appreciated to some extent by uncultivated hearers, and it is full of points of beauty that are easily understood. While the opening theme of the *allegro non troppo*, $\frac{3}{4}$ time, is among the most easily assimilated things of Brahms, its component parts, the bass-crotchets of the opening bar, the exquisite melody for horns and bassoons built on the notes of the tonic harmony, and the rising phrase in flutes, clarinets, and bassoons, are one and all used in the development of the movement with wonderful skill; yet the delivery of the theme in which they occur is as simple as something of Mozart.

A violin passage, reminding us in its suavity of a similar phrase in the overture to the *Erste Walpurgisnacht* of Mendelssohn, is also important in the development, and the second subject, into which it leads (given out by violas and violoncellos in F sharp minor), is accompanied by a figure on the violins which afterwards gains great prominence. There is plenty of more vigorous music even before we reach the double-bar, and the working-out section is of magnificent quality. Throughout the movement we are surprised at the wealth of thematic material that is lavished upon it; it is all generated from the initial themes, but many of the episodical melodies strike us as unconnected with anything that has gone before. The coda of the movement is perhaps the most thrilling thing in the symphony. Over the rhythmic pulsations of the strings, *pizzicato*, appear the various episodes, and at last the horns, this time with trumpets, repeat the first subject with which they began. At the beginning of the adagio in B major [1] a rising passage on the bassoon is associated with a falling phrase on the violoncello, which begins a serene and lovely melody of considerable length; a middle

[1] It is curious to notice the succession of keys in the first two symphonies; in the C minor, the successive movements rise by a major third each time, C minor, E major, A flat major, and C being the keys; in the second symphony the key relations are in the reverse order, in a descending series of thirds, the first movement being in D, the second in B, the third in G, and the last, of course, in D.

section in $\frac{12}{8}$ contrasts with this, and at the resumption of the former time, the triplet figures left over as it were, from the middle section, are used in the accompaniment, and are finally allowed to die away gradually in the drums. The third movement, an *allegretto grazioso*, in G, $\frac{3}{4}$ time, has a kind of rustic simplicity about it, the oboes, clarinets, and bassoons, the bumpkins of the orchestra, having the opening theme above a *pizzicato* accompaniment on the violoncello. Contrast is made by transforming the theme into a gay, excitable little theme in $\frac{2}{4}$ time, *presto*, which peeps out suddenly with an air of childish mischief that is quite irresistible. Another *presto*, $\frac{3}{8}$, interrupts this and leads to the reappearance of the first theme in the key of F sharp, a device of a kind most rarely employed by Brahms; the modulation through B, back to G major, is deftly managed. The final *allegro con spirito* is a little square-cut and conventional after the rest of the lovely work; but its second subject has some of the joyful bigness that was such a typical quality in Brahms's nature and in his music. Rapid quaver scales in thirds on the various wood-wind instruments are a characteristic feature of the movement, which from the entry of the second subject never loses its interest for a moment.

The first two symphonies are divided from the last two by two concertos and two overtures among the orchestral works. Op. 77, the violin concerto, is in D, and its opening has much of the suavity of the second symphony, apart from the theme being, as there, built on the successive notes of the tonic harmony. Brahms goes back to the tradition of the older concerto-form, giving a long exposition of the material of the first movement before the entry of the solo instrument. When the violin does come in, it is with a kind of breathless passage, on which there was some discussion between the composer and Joachim.[1]

We cannot fail to trace in the passages for solo the special points in which Joachim was without a rival, such as the handling of several parts and other things. The absence of the slightest trace of passages written for mere effect is as characteristic of the player as of the composer; and, like the other concertos, the work for violin is to be judged first and foremost as a composition, not as a means of display. Occasionally it may have happened that in the desire to avoid the meretricious, Brahms allowed himself to make the violin part so harsh as almost to repel the general public at first; even in the short time since the death of Joachim, who was, of course, unrivalled in it, the work has come increasingly into favour with violinists, and nowadays even the prodigies are bold enough to attempt it. M. Ysaye, whose sympathies must be altogether with another school of music, has given a strange reading of it, which does not throw much light on Brahms's intentions; Herr Kreisler's performance of it stands alone in its superb ease and command of resource. The working of the second subject with its dotted rhythms, and of a figure introduced later by the soloist of two semiquavers and a quaver, is of the utmost skill and interest, and in the cadenza—which, again following old custom, Brahms leaves to the performer—it is doubtless right to resume the consideration of all of them, as was done in the noble

[1] On the whole question of Joachim's influence on the work, see the *Joachim Correspondence*, vol. i. pp. 139–57. A footnote on p. 147 points out how ready Brahms was to accept his friend's suggestions in points of structure or form, and how unwilling to take the hints the great violinist gave him in matters of technical difficulty and the like. The whole incident throws a charming light on the relation of the two men.

cadenza which Joachim was accustomed to play. At the opening of the *adagio*, in F major, the wood-wind and horns accompany the first oboe in a melody of the most unmistakably Brahmsian origin. It is built on the successive notes of the tonic chord, and its geniality, gentle pathos, and artless beauty are enhanced by the instrument on which it is given out. It is curious that, except for a reference to the first three notes of this tune, the solo violin never plays it, all the prominent solo passages being in vigorous contrast to it, or else an accompaniment of descending octave figures. One of the most romantic things in the world is the ending to the movement, in which the violin, starting with syncopations that give the effect of hardly restrained sobs, finally soars up to the heights on an arpeggio figure. The finale, *allegro giocoso*, has an unmistakably Hungarian flavour about it, as if a dedication to the great Hungarian violinist were conveyed in it. Its strongly rhythmical first subject is contrasted with a theme of rising octaves in a dotted rhythm, and towards the end a remarkable gravity is imparted into the section by a polyphonic passage for the solo instrument, which gradually spreads to the other strings and thence to the rest of the orchestra. The cadenza of this movement is a mere flourish, and is written out in full.

Brahms very often wrote, or at least published, his compositions in pairs, the one forming an artistic counterpart and complement to the other. The instances of this habit are too numerous to point out in detail; it has been often referred to by commentators on his work. As the first two symphonies came within a year of each other, and the third and fourth within two years of each other, so the two overtures which are next to be considered, Opp. 80 and 81, made their appearance together, and at the earlier perform-

BRAHMS CONDUCTING

FROM A DRAWING BY PROF. W. VON BECKERATH

ances were played in the same programme. The first, *Akademische Fest-Ouvertüre*, is a work of the utmost jollity, the *Tragische Ouvertüre* of the utmost solemnity and grandeur; as though the master were anxious to keep the balance between the two extremes before himself as well as before his hearers. The first of the two was an acknowledgment of, not an exercise for, the degree of Dr. Phil. conferred on the composer by the University of Breslau in 1880, and was performed there on 4 January, 1881, the other overture having been played in the previous month at the Vienna Philharmonic. The *Academic* overture might stand as an eternal refutation of all that is meant by that misused adjective in the mouths of a section of modern critics. Anything less "academic," in their sense, it would be impossible to imagine. It is university life from the student's point of view, and four of the best students' songs of Germany are introduced into it with extraordinary effect and ingenuity: *Wir hatten gebauet ein stättliches Haus*, *Hört' ich sing*, *Was kommt dort von der Höh'?* (the "Fuchslied," or Freshman's song), and last of all, the famous *Gaudeamus igitur*, which makes a splendid climax. The first of the tunes, as well as the last, is given out with a good deal of pomp, and the hilarity of the whole is never for a moment lacking in dignity, unless we except the passage where the bassoon has the theme of the "Fuchslied," a touch of colour which would have struck English people as especially funny if the bassoon joke had not been done to death in the majority of the operas of Sullivan. The use of the viola in the delivery of the broad theme in F major, the use of the three trumpets later on, and the rushing violin scales which accompany the *Gaudeamus igitur*, are surely evidence that the composer had a sense of orchestral colour.

The other overture tempts us by its name to attach some particular story to it; but as might be expected from so great a master, it is indeed lost labour to guess at any definite tragedy. It opens ominously, although in the major mode; the suggestions on oboe, bassoon, etc., of the theme that is afterwards uttered with such wonderful effect by the trombones, gives the effect of a hush of expectation. When the tragic character is fully realized, the music seems to nerve us to new efforts, but the resumption of the ominous opening tells us that these too are in vain; the *molto più moderato* hints at a quiet, brave resumption of ordinary duties after some crushing blow has fallen. A wonderful passage occurs (p. 50 of the score), where the horns appropriate the ominous phrase, but play it in half time, changing its final notes with poignant effect. Perhaps "tragic" is scarcely the word for a work which, while realizing all the sadness of life, yet sends the hearer away all the stronger for having heard it.

Op. 83, the second concerto for pianoforte and orchestra, is in B flat, and came out in 1882. It is a work of the amplest proportions and of the utmost difficulty; there are four movements instead of the three almost universally found in concertos, the fourth (the second in order) being, so it is said, added because the composer thought the first allegro was too simple. Simplicity is not the characteristic which most people detect in this first movement, for, apart from its thematic beauty, its unusual structure is apt to puzzle even educated hearers at first. The essential part of it is a phrase given out by the horn alone and answered by a fine pianoforte flourish, at the end of which the horn-phrase is echoed; there is after this a long preliminary passage for piano alone before the proper entry of the theme, which is soon subjected to all kinds of treatment before the second subject enters, and when it does it is never allowed to occupy the chief place, our attention being confined to the first phrase and its resultant episodes almost all through. The scherzo in D minor looks back to the first serenade, Op. 11, for the shape of its theme, though there is no further resemblance. It is far clearer in outline than the first movement, and its lovely second theme with its truly "pianistic" treatment haunts the ear long after it is done. A very difficult passage of stealthy octaves in both hands *sotto voce* for the solo instrument, and a spirited martial measure in which sudden triumph is suggested, are among the most striking moments in this elaborate movement; the *andante* in B flat is of extreme beauty, and the delivery of its theme by a violoncello solo, afterwards taken up by bassoon and first violin, is an interesting touch of colour. It is curious that the solo instrument is not allowed to play this lovely tune (compare the slow movement of the violin concerto), but is required to embroider it with wonderfully effective and almost Chopinesque passages. It is allowed a few bars of exceedingly effective music for a close to the section. The final *allegretto grazioso* reminds us a little of the last movement of the violin concerto, being in the same time, $\frac{2}{4}$, and having much of the same kind of exuberant gaiety. There are subordinate subjects of great beauty and individuality, such as that which, first appearing in A minor, seems to bring back the period of the Hungarian dances, and the gently hovering subject which soon follows it in B flat major. The essential features of the main theme are transformed into what is virtually $\frac{6}{8}$ time in the *poco più presto* that ushers in the close of the movement. It is not, of course, for every pianist, even for those whose technique is sufficient for it;

for it needs a special degree of insight and sympathy to interpret it properly, and enormous staying power is demanded from the soloist. The conductor, too, must be able to bring out the proper balance between the piano and the orchestra, and to make one subordinate to the other as is required. Otherwise, however skilful the playing, the work will baffle ordinary hearers as much by its newness of tone-effects as by the unconventionality of its structure.

The third symphony, in F, Op. 90, appeared in 1884, and it is not too much to say that it forms the final culmination of the classical symphonic form developed along the lines laid down before Beethoven, and carried in his first eight symphonies to heights of emotional power unguessed at by those who created it. The ninth symphony of Beethoven, and the fourth of Brahms, like many other works by composers of the romantic and later schools, are not under discussion just now, as in these there are attempts to extend the classical form in various directions. But the third symphony of Brahms, in so far as it extends the classical form, does so along the lines of its natural growth, and it may be said that no work exists of any date which more gloriously establishes the wealth of the form, and its fitness for the purpose. Some concession is indeed made to those who hold that the thematic material of the various parts of the symphony should be closely related throughout; for there are cases where the themes recur in a most interesting way in movements to which they do not properly belong. The opening "motto" on one of those incomplete arpeggios so beloved of the master consists of the chord of F minor, given out by wood-wind and trumpets, the rising notes F, A flat, and the upper F being prominent. It is tempting to follow Herr Kalbeck [1] in his assumption that here again we have an allusion to the motto "Frei, aber froh!" though the actual form of the middle note is not A, but "As." At the third bar, the double bassoon has the three notes in double length, while the real first subject of the movement is F given out by the violins, a descending passage coming from the high F. Just before the second subject appears, there occurs one of the rare instances in which Brahms has used phrases first uttered by another composer, for the harmonies and melodic phrase of this

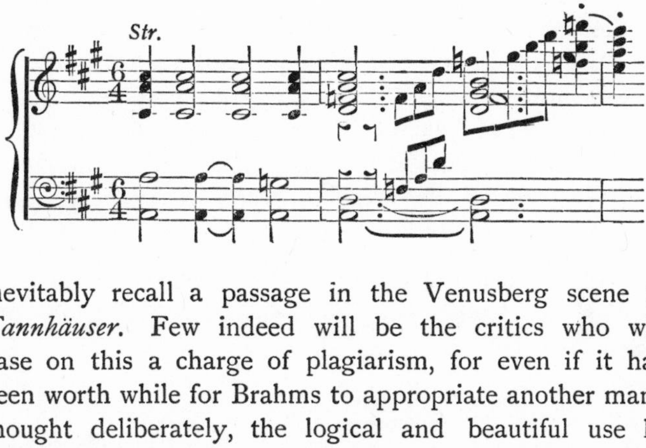

inevitably recall a passage in the Venusberg scene in *Tannhäuser*. Few indeed will be the critics who will base on this a charge of plagiarism, for even if it had been worth while for Brahms to appropriate another man's thought deliberately, the logical and beautiful use he makes of it in the place where he puts it would be enough to exonerate him. As a matter of fact, it can be nothing but the merest coincidence. The second subject in the unusual key of A major is of exquisite suavity and amenity, and its rhythm soon yields a new figure of two staccato notes which is destined to become of great importance. Soon our minds are carried back to the opening "motto" of the whole, and matters of graver import lead

[1] i. 102.

to the repetition of the first half of the movement. According to later usage in the classical form, the working-out and recapitulation sections are combined, the second subject reappearing this time in D major, and the whole of the thematic material being elaborately developed in a way which makes the movement remarkable for its interest even among Brahms's greatest works. The sedate and square-cut theme of the andante in C is given out by the clarinets and bassoons, and in its third bar, and particularly in the echo of that bar in which the strings are led by the viola, we may surely trace the influence of the "motto" theme of the opening. In like manner, the two staccato notes which had their source in the second subject of the allegro start the strongly emotional second theme of the slow movement, and in the course of discussion occurs this wonderful piece of bold suspension and resolution of dissonances. The

parentage of a beautiful passage in which the meaning of the movement is summed up, is not quite clear at once, but the rhythm of the main subject is no doubt its first suggestion, and from this point to the end of the section, with the resumption of the bold dissonances, and of the main theme in a slightly altered guise so as to convey a deeper poetry, the movement reaches a wonderfully effective ending. The third movement, *poco allegretto*, is the best of a large group of creations of Brahms which have been discussed elsewhere; one of his most individual moods was that of a gentle melancholy, often associated with a playful figure, and touching none of the deeper springs of human emotion, but rather suggesting some half-human creature, some weeping dryad or disconsolate fairy.

The violoncello has the exquisitely graceful theme in C minor, and the other strings accompany in light arpeggio figures, the wood-wind joining in gradually. The structure of this, and of the trio section, in which the wood-wind have a sort of waltz-theme, with syncopated accompaniment on the violoncello, is as simple as Mozart, and on the return of the first theme its delivery on the horn adds picturesqueness to the whole. The final allegro in F minor—a movement which suggested to Joachim the idea of Hero and Leander [1]—begins with a creeping subject that is full of suspense, and it is soon arrested by the two reiterated notes on trombones, which remind us of the first and slow movements; though this time they usher in a new and eloquent theme, or rather episode. The second subject proper is a swinging triplet theme in C (Leander, according to Joachim), given to the horns and violoncellos,

[1] See *Joachim Correspondence*, ii. 19.

and emphasized by being the first occurrence of any but square time. How the main theme is dissected, presented in changed aspects, in fragments, and in conjunction with the other themes, there is not space to tell. Its most wonderful transformation occurs near the close, at the *poco sostenuto*, which serves as a coda to the whole symphony. The oboe has the theme in long notes, and after two bars the first phrase is suddenly turned into the major and taken up by the flute over a quasi-tremolando figure on the upper strings.

Soon the reiterated chords are joined with the string-figure, and quite at the end a final and joyful surprise is reserved for us, the first (descending) theme of the opening allegro being suggested rather than distinctly heard at the top of the wavering figure in the first violin part. There are many Brahms lovers who regard this third symphony as the crowning point of the master's work, at least as far as orchestral music is concerned ; for this cause, perhaps, it is at present almost more rarely given than any of the others. It is so warm in colouring and so effectively scored that it might have been expected to appeal to those with whom such qualities are paramount.

The fourth symphony, in E minor, Op. 98, came out in 1886, and at once gave rise to much discussion because of the innovation in its final movement. In many ways it is in strong contrast with the third symphony, for its themes are as a rule presented in shorter and more rudimentary guise at first, as the mere germs of what is to follow. A figure of two notes played by violins is the seed from which the first subject of the *allegro non troppo* is made, and the subject is not one of those that make the most immediate appeal to the audience ; nor is the second subject very striking at first, though the little figure which introduces it, for horns and wood-wind, arrests attention ; it is not for its thematic value, but for the marvellous ingenuity and mastery of its development that the movement is so highly esteemed. The *andante moderato* is professedly in E major, but the opening on the horns treats the real keynote as the third of the key of C, so that we are deluded for a time into thinking the section is to be in that key. The theme is strongly emotional, and although it is in the major, the remembrance of the introductory bars gives a kind of undefined minor touch to it which makes for plaintive effect. It is carried out at considerable length, and, as Mr. Colles says, "It approaches very nearly to full first-movement form, since there is a second subject which first appears in B major and afterwards in the tonic key." At its appearance in the tonic key this second subject is played on the strings divided into eight parts, with beautiful quiet richness of sound. The third movement *allegro giocoso*, in C major, is again in a form closely assimilated to that of the typical first movement; there is a fine coda, with a persistent drum-passage, but as a whole the movement is perhaps the least interesting part of the symphony, and its note of hilarity sometimes makes it seem a little wanting in distinction. The last movement, after these three sections in more or less close conformity to the symphonic first-movement type, breaks entirely new ground, for though the passacaglia and the chaconne, those two nearly allied forms, had been used freely in the eighteenth century (the chaconne was at one time an almost indispensable ending to every opera), yet they had never before come into the symphonic scheme, and the last instance of their employment by the great masters was probably the set of thirty-two variations in C minor by Beethoven. It is of the essence of the best type of the chaconne, passacaglia, or "ground"—to give it its old English name—that the repetitions of the simple and constantly recurring theme should be made to flow into one another so as to create a feeling of unity and rising climax; so in the three sections of Bach's chaconne for violin alone, each group of variations on the theme rises to its own culmination and carries the hearer's attention on, so that he forgets the reiteration of the underlying succession of notes. Of this form, which, in weaker hands, was apt to degenerate into an unrelated series of mechanical variations, there never was a treatment so strongly unified as the finale of Brahms's last symphony. The theme is of eight notes, and its repetitions in one guise or another are exactly continuous almost throughout the movement, though it is pretty safe to say that no hearer unaccustomed to the work ever yet followed them from beginning to end without getting puzzled at certain points. The interest of what is built on the theme is so great that the ear can only with difficulty remember the succession of notes that lie at the root of the whole, and, once lost, their sequence is very difficult to recall. It is not a movement for the great public, at all events for the present; whether the people at large will unconsciously acquire the skill to follow it without assistance from the printed book or programme, cannot as yet be said; but when we remember that experiments in form which, when Schumann's works were new, puzzled the professional writers of English programmes, are now accepted and delighted in by uneducated working-people, we feel that nothing is impossible in the way of human development. One of the hardest places to follow is where, at the thirteenth repetition, the time changes from $\frac{3}{4}$ with a note of the theme to each bar, to $\frac{3}{2}$ where the flute has a highly ornamental version of the theme over a persistent bass. At the seventeenth repetition the subject is once more presented as clearly as at the beginning, and we start again; after the thirty-second repetition there are four intercalary bars which lead to a coda *più allegro*, in which the theme is treated rather more freely, and the exact division into groups of eight bars is no longer maintained. The student should not fail to read the interesting series of letters on this symphony which passed between the composer and Frau von Herzogenberg.[1]

One more work in which orchestra was employed remained for Brahms to write, the concerto for violin and violoncello in A minor, Op. 102, written for his friends, Joseph Joachim and Robert Hausmann, who played it, as need hardly be said, with incomparable beauty of style. While the instruments are closely welded into the general structure of the work, there are not wanting passages of display, such as the fine opening cadenza for the two solo instruments, and their passage in full harmony together. The vigorous theme of the opening *allegro* and the delicious second subject given at first to the violoncello, must strike even those hearers who are not unnaturally puzzled by the unusual character and colouring of the piece, in which the main contrast is between the orchestra and the two soloists playing together and often creating the impression as of a string quartet. The loveliness of the slow movement is irresistible, and from the graceful curve of its main subject to the coda all is full of beauty and poetical meaning. In the last movement there is a return

[1] See the *Herzogenberg Correspondence*, ii. 89 ff.; trans., 243 ff.; and the *Joachim Correspondence*, ii. 208–12; also Litzmann's *Clara Schumann*, iii. 472.

to Brahms's favourite gipsy music, which is inevitably suggested in the rhythm of the opening, announced by the violoncello.[1] It is curious to see how prominent is the part given to the lower solo instrument throughout the concerto, and here again both subjects are at first allotted to the violoncello. There is a remarkable wealth of thematic material in the movement, and the writing for the soloists is so full that in more than one passage the effect of a string sextet is given by both violin and violoncello having passages of triple-stopping. The piece cannot be played by ordinary virtuosi, who fail to lift it from its obscurities as great artists do. The two great interpreters for whom it was written, though both are now departed, have left the traditions of their readings behind them, and it is these, rather than any words or examples, which will throw light on a work which may very possibly be long in entering into its due share of appreciation.

[1] On the bowing of the chief subject, see the *Joachim Correspondence*, i. 220, and on certain other technical points in the first movement, ii. 230.

BRAHMS CONDUCTING

FROM A DRAWING BY PROF. W. VON BECKERATH

CHAPTER VII

THE SONGS

BEFORE examining the songs of Brahms in detail, it is necessary to keep in mind the broad divisions which German musicians recognize in classifying lyrics for a single voice. Of all the classes there are numerous examples in our master's work, and there is no evidence that at any time of his life he preferred one class to another.

First, the "Volkslied" is a genuine product of the art of a nation, owning no individual creator, but reckoned as the spontaneous outcome of the people. It is not necessary to discuss the vexed question of the authorship of these melodies, which exist in all countries and in all periods of artistic history. In many cases the tunes, like the words, may have been gradually modified or enlarged to suit the purposes of the humble singers by whom they were transmitted, and they exist in many slightly different forms, possessing the common characteristic that, with a few exceptions, the original composer is unknown to the world. The few exceptions are (so far as Germany is concerned) those in which the original purpose of the tune has been altered, like Isaac's *Ispruck, ich muss dich lassen,* which was soon adapted to sacred words, and became one of the most solemn and universally beloved of chorales. The modern composer's work in regard to these is to arrange them and their accompaniments in such a way as to bring out their natural beauty as fully as may be, in order that his contemporaries may realize the simple charm of the melody. Hence the simpler the form of accompaniment, and of the harmonic scheme, the better as a general rule. Musical artifice of any kind is usually to be eschewed altogether, or if employed at all it must almost necessarily be for the sake of laying stress on some change in the character of the words.

The second class is that of the "Volksthümliches Lied," in which the tune is the invention of the composer, but conforms more or less strictly to the type of real folk-song. There is obviously great scope here for the art of an imaginative musician to fit his theme so closely to the expression of the words that it may seem as spontaneous as a folk-song, while greater freedom is allowed in the matter of harmonic setting.

The third class, in which, as in the two former, the same melody recurs for every stanza of the poem, is known as the "Strophisches Lied," differing mainly from songs of the second class in its wider divergence from the folk-song type, and in still greater plasticity in regard to harmony.

In the fourth class, that of the "Durchcomponirtes Lied,"[1] the composer is at full liberty to follow the minute changes in the poem, without regard to the melody that may be set to the opening words. It is clear that this class may be far more highly organized than the others, although the earliest examples, dating from the times of Caccini and his

[1] It is a serious drawback that there are no recognized English equivalents for these two terms. "Volksthümlich" may be paraphrased as "after the manner of a folk-song"; "Durchcomponirt"—"through-composed"—can only be expressed in some such roundabout way as "a song with different music for every verse."

Nuove Musiche, when the strict musical forms of the sixteenth century were abandoned in order to obtain greater and more definite expressiveness in musical utterance, contain hardly any germs of musical organism. Caccini, Monteverde, and the other Italians of their times, Schütz and the Germans before Bach, Henry Lawes and the English masters before Purcell, reveal hardly any system of musical design other than the purpose of following as faithfully as possible the accentuation of the words they set. There is not really as much difference as would appear between the ideals aimed at in this class of song and those of the other three classes; for it is to be supposed that the unknown author or authors of a folk-song got the first hint of their melody from the rhythmic accentuation of the first verse of the primitive poem, and in some cases the writers of folk-song words no doubt adapted their utterances to the rhythm and character of a pre-existing tune, even as in later days Scott, Burns, Thomas Moore, and subsequent bards, in setting new words to old tunes, have received their first inspiration from the swing of the tunes themselves. While it is quite clear that several different stanzas of poetry, sung to the same melody, cannot all be expected to fit it as closely as the first verse, yet true accentuation may often be found in a "strophic" song or in a folk-song. Nor is a composer's preference of one or other of the earlier classes of this enumeration to be construed into a disregard on his part of the need for just accentuation, or "declamation" as it is often called, in setting words that must be fitted to new music as they pass. Music, too, is an art so highly organized, that such attempts as those of Caccini in Italy or Lawes in England are to be regarded as essentially spasmodic; the human ear desires recurrence of musical ideas, and such phenomena as these were inevitably followed by a return to more or less formal music in which accentuation is only one of several objects. Of the great classical song-writers, Haydn, in his canzonets, seems to have been the first who contrived to put organic life and thematic continuity into the "Durchcomponirtes Lied"; Beethoven, in *Wonne der Wehmuth*, and occasionally elsewhere, combined perfect accentuation with a symmetrical musical design; Schubert, like Mozart, can seldom forgo his love of formal symmetry in his exquisite melodies, and in his "declamatory" songs the long passages in which there is true accentuation of the words usually give place, sooner or later, to a formal tune repeated over and over in the "strophic" manner; the plan of the whole is virtually identical with the "cantatas" of an older day, in which formal airs are separated by the driest of recitatives. At present, the ultra-modern school of song-writers, from Duparc and César Franck to Debussy and Ravel in France, and from Hugo Wolf to Max Reger in Germany, while they never sacrifice the accentuation of the words to any purely musical consideration, are yet apt to give a certain continuity to their songs by means of a figure of accompaniment. In the very earliest group of the songs of Brahms, we find instances of this way of attaining musical unity in spite of the fact that the vocal part depends upon nothing but the accentuation of the words. He is often as bold in this way as Wagner was in works written long after these, when his early style had been replaced by one in which the words, freely declaimed, are relieved against a background of marvellous richness and intricacy. It was not by a mere happy accident that the literary standard of the words set by Brahms was always so remarkably high. He paid the closest attention to this matter, and was accustomed to write out poems which took his fancy in note-books carried about in his pocket.[1]

Taking now the earliest group of Brahms's songs, those of the years 1853–8, comprising Opp. 3, 6, and 7, the single song *Mondnacht*, and the *Volkskinderlieder* arranged for the children of Robert and Clara Schumann (without opus-number, and the latter without the arranger's name), we find specimens of all the types just described. The last group consists of fourteen of the most charming of German nursery songs, such as *Sandmännchen*, *Marienwürmchen*, *Schlaf', Kindlein, schlaf'*, arranged with the utmost simplicity, yet with occasional admission of musical ingenuity, as in the accompaniment of *Sandmännchen* or the pretty moving bass of *Das Mädchen und die Hasel.* Nothing could be more truly "volksthümlich" than the *Volkslied* and *Trauernde* of Op. 7, and the song that stands first of all Brahms's vocal works, *Liebestreu*, Op. 3, No. 1, is of matchless eloquence among "strophic" songs, the emotion of the passion illustrated rising with irresistible power to the climax, though the means used are of the simplest, merely a gradual acceleration of the speed, and a change to the tonic major in the third verse. The second of the same series, *Wie sich Rebenranken schwingen*, is "durchcomponirt," but its thirty-three bars contain a minute set of variations on a theme at first given out in unison, treated canonically in the third and fourth lines, as a bass in the second verse, with a new theme in the vocal part,[2] while

[1] Kalbeck, i. 100.

[2] Kalbeck finds in this new theme, which may be held to recur in the third song of the set, a quotation from Mozart's *Batti, batti.* It may have been intentional, as he suggests, but the fact that it is a somewhat self-evident contrapuntal corollary to the theme itself surely points to a musical rather than to a poetical purpose (see *Life*, i. 159).

in the coda, set to the last couplet repeated, the original theme is sung in notes of twice the original value, with the new theme in the accompaniment. This minute analysis of the song is of course not meant as direct evidence of the composer's greatness, for feats of ingenuity have often, as we all know, been made to hide defects of real inspiration; but in this case the expression of the song is spontaneous and direct, and the ingenuity is so finely subordinated to the general effect that it might easily escape notice. The next, *Ich muss hinaus*, has a splendidly ardent theme on a rising scale, which returns at the close, after a gentler section in which a theme suggested by the words, "Ich will die Rosen nicht mehr sehn," is worked with the finest skill. The fourth of the set, *Weit über das Feld*, is, like the first, strophic, with the exception of a slight intensification of the melody at the close; but all through the accentuation of the words is as careful as though the song were "durchcomponirt." In *In der Fremde*, as in the single song, *Mondnacht*, published separately in 1854, Brahms has here reset words identified with Schumann's most beautiful music; and in both songs Schumann, we may freely admit, has the best of it. The sixth of the set, *Lindes Rauschen in den Wipfeln*, is "durchcomponirt," the main theme returning for the close, after a short section of beautiful poetic and musical contrast. It is not without interest to students of literary history that this first set of songs was dedicated to Bettina von Arnim, the friend of Goethe, to whom Beethoven addressed some impassioned letters.

The next set, Op. 6, begins with a *Spanisches Lied* to words by Paul Heyse, with many Spanish characteristics in it; among the next four, in "strophic" form, are *Der Frühling*, with an ardour that makes it redolent of spring, and *Juchhe!* on a motive of hunting-horns, and with short interludes built on the theme of the song in diminution (*i.e.*, in notes of half the original value); the sixth, *Nachtigallen schwingen*, with its exciting accompaniment, is the first of a type of songs in which Brahms has no rival, and which rise from a vivid picture of a natural scene to strong human emotion.

Treue Liebe and *Parole*, with which Op. 7 opens, are strophic songs of great beauty, the first giving a prophecy of *Verzagen* in its figure of accompaniment suggesting the surf breaking on a desolate shore; *Anklänge* is a haunting little picture of a girl spinning the thread for a wedding garment which the hearer knows she will never wear, although the foreboding is nowhere but in the music. The last, *Heimkehr*, is a short gush of expectant emotion with beautiful and unobtrusive use of the thematic germ of the prelude.

In 1861–2 appeared two more sets of songs, which show the composer as on the threshold of his great lyrical masterpieces. Though they can hardly rank among his best songs, and though their comparative neglect in the past is easy to account for, yet from the point of view of the later achievements they are not only worthy of study, but actually effective for practical use when sung before an audience that is familiar with the characteristics of the composer. Op. 14, published in 1861, has eight songs, several of which are inscribed "Volkslied," the term clearly referring to the words rather than to the music. In the first, *Vor dem Fenster*, the strophic form is preserved, but in the fourth verse a wonderful effect as of a sudden burst of sunlight is produced by nothing more elaborate than a change to the major mode and an upper vocal part that soars above the melody. *Vom verwundeten Knaben*,

Gang zur Liebsten, and *Sehnsucht*, show, in melody and accompaniment, a feeling for the austerity of style that marks the best folk-songs, but the *Sonett*—to thirteenth-century words—is singularly direct in its expressiveness. *Trennung* and *Ständchen* are vigorous, and both have charming figures of accompaniment, the latter being in some ways suggestive of Schubert's *Hark, hark, the lark*. *Murray's Ermordung* has plenty of force, but is less directly eloquent than the later songs on similar subjects, such as *Edward* or *Entführung*.

Five songs make up Op. 19: *Der Kuss*,[1] with a flowing melody of five-bar rhythm; *Scheiden und Meiden* and *In der Ferne*, a pair of songs built on the same strange phrase with its wide intervals of open fifths, and each serving as the complement of the other; *Der Schmied*, that superb picture of a girl's pride in her lover's strength, which is founded on a theme of obviously realistic suggestion (a part-song of Schumann's, from his Op. 145, may have brought Uhland's words under the notice of Brahms, and it is instructive to compare the earlier master's rather tentative way of conveying the swinging rhythm with the latter's boldness and certainty of handling); and, last, the exquisitely romantic *An eine Aeolsharfe*, in which the characteristic effect of the instrument is beautifully conveyed.

The nine songs of Op. 32 are so arranged in order as to set the last in the best possible light. This, the lovely *Wie bist du, meine Königin*, comes as a most welcome climax of obvious beauty after various intense emotions have been portrayed; for in this set we are shown the deeper things of human feeling, and the pictures of various moods are drawn with wonderful skill. The first, *Wie*

[1] On the accentuation of this song, see Kalbeck, i. 342.

rafft ich mich auf in der Nacht, is a striking example of the use of thematic development, the rhythmic figure begotten of the opening words being used throughout in the accompaniment. The repetition of the words, "in der Nacht," by poet and musician gives the note of feverish restlessness which well introduces the halting accents of *Nicht mehr zu dir zu gehen*, the plaintive *Ich schleich' umher*, and the anxious questions of *Der Strom, der neben mir verrauschte, wo ist er nun?* always asked in a rising phrase.

The peculiar effect of *Wehe, so willst du mich wieder*, ending on a note of rapture, is undoubtedly got by the bold and frequent modulations employed through the short song. The three following are studies of lovers' disagreements, which in music might serve as parallels to some of Browning's shorter and more intimate poems. In the final song of the set (*Wie bist du, meine Königin*) we seem obliged to admit that there is some truth in the charges of occasional faulty accentuation laid to the door of Brahms; the melodic opening phrase allows of no break at the point where the comma would warn the reader of the words that a break must be made; the heaviest accents fall on the first syllable of "meine" and the last of "Königin,"

and, after the first line, where it is essential that the words should run on to complete the sentence, there is a break in the musical phrase. It is not till we get to the recurrence of the phrase in the second stanza that we feel the perfect fitness of the words and music to each other; and at the final verse it is clear that the words have themselves suggested the musical phrase. This will be easily seen by comparing the two verbal phrases, in respect of their adaptation to the same musical theme. Hard indeed must be the heart, and dull the hearing, of any pedant who should resist the appeal of the lovely song on account of a momentary infraction of a rule which Brahms elsewhere shows himself most careful to observe. For the song, from the first note to the last, is one of the immortal lyrics of the world, and it is quite clear that the musical theme could not have been so twisted and changed as to provide an ideal musical equivalent for the opening words, without a sacrifice of absolute musical beauty which we may well imagine that Brahms was reluctant to make. And if new music had been made for the opening verse, the phrase at the climax would have lost its point, for it must come in as a remembrance, not as a subject heard for the first time. The song, besides being, in the word of the refrain, "wonnevoll" in the highest sense, is especially interesting in the matter of form, for it belongs to a type which Brahms uses more frequently than almost any other, and which unites some characteristics of the "strophic" and the "durchcomponirt" classes. Verses one, two, and four are set to the same strain (with a slight harmonic change in the fourth, but the other two having identically the same music); the third shows considerable thematic alteration and even development, so that the whole scheme is a kind of miniature version of the classical sonata-form, but built on a single theme instead of on two contrasting subjects. The sections of the form, viz., statement, repetition, development, and recapitulation, here correspond with the four stanzas of the poem.

The set of fifteen romances from Tieck's *Magelone*, which make up Op. 33, stand entirely by themselves in the history of song-writing. Though many of them illustrate moments in the story that are more or less dramatic, not one has any trace of dramatic treatment, and the passage, so full of suggestion for the average dramatic composer, where Pierre feels himself called in one direction by the song of the Sultan's daughter, and in another by the remembrance of the fair Magelone, is not musically illustrated at all. There is not even an attempt at local colour, nor is Sulima's song any more oriental in character than the rest. The gallant *Traun! Bogen und Pfeil* has a vigour that suits knightly energy, but it is not especially characteristic of the age of chivalry. The songs may lack some of the qualities which ordinary people would expect in lyrics illustrating a story, but they have merits that outweigh those qualities. In listening to them we feel that the conventional knight and lady of the old romance, and of Tieck's version, are mere puppets, but that the human emotions are so vividly portrayed in the songs that we willingly forget the costumes and even the incidents of the story. The explanation of the strange incongruity between the Wardour Street romance and the deeply spiritual moods of the songs may be found perhaps in the fact that the story, in the version of Marbach, was one of the composer's favourite books at a very impressionable time of his life; he read it with his girl-friend and pupil, Lischen Giesemann, when he was fourteen and she thirteen, and no doubt it kept its charm for him until the day when he gave the poems a new glamour for the rest of the world. In form, several of the songs are on a new pattern, that of an extended lyric, often passing into a fresh rhythm, altering the rate of speed, and introducing new thematic material. The songs are not connected with each other by any identity or even similarity of subject; there is no effort to bind them together by "leit-motives" or any device of that kind; and while all are removed into an impersonal sphere where the story matters as little as the aspect of the characters represented, in all, or almost all, the height of lyric utterance is touched. Each has its own climax, arrived at with every appearance of spontaneity; and for this reason, even more than for the circumstance that the songs are divided among four characters (a minstrel, Magelone, and Sulima having one each, and Pierre the remainder), the set of songs does not make a very effective cycle when performed in its entirety. The first, the minstrel's song, with its trotting figure of accompaniment, is an example of the composer's power of keeping up the interest of one long continuous movement on a single theme; the second, *Traun! Bogen und Pfeil*, has already been mentioned; the third, *Sind es Schmerzen, sind es Freuden*, in which the dawn of love in the knight's heart at first sight of the beloved is described, from the first almost awe-struck uncertainty to the rapture of conviction, is in four movements, the last being virtually identical with the second. The next, the lovely *Liebe kam aus fernen Landen*, and the vigorous *So willst du des Armen*, are more conventional in design, but both are among the most intimate and characteristic of Brahms's songs; the sixth, *Wiè soll ich die Freude*, starts with a spirited theme carried out by voice and accompaniment with masterly skill of development; at the words "Schlage, sehnsüchtige Gewalt," a noble subject in triple time enters and is thoroughly and beautifully worked; after a brief resumption of the first theme, a new movement, *vivace ma non troppo*, reaches the height of exultation, and at the close the original subject is again resumed. A shorter song in one section, *War es dir, dem diese Lippen bebten*, leads to another of the greater songs of the set, in which the knight takes leave of his lute on the eve of the successful elopement; *Wir müssen uns trennen, geliebtes Saitenspiel*, is in a happily elegiac mood, and with a reference to his weapons a strenuous allegro begins, carried to greater length than usual in *da capo* songs, to which class the resumption of the original measure shows it to belong. Next, while his lady sleeps, Pierre sings to her the magically beautiful lullaby, *Ruhe, Süssliebchen*, in which the accompaniment seems to be provided by gently waving branches. Those who may wish to know by what very improbable means the lovers are separated, and Pierre twice over finds himself in an open boat alone at sea, are recommended to read the summary of the story given in the appendix to vol. i. of Miss May's *Life of Brahms.* The first of Pierre's marine adventures gives the suggestion of *Verzweiflung*, which, like the other, *Wie froh und frisch*, is purely the expression of a mental or spiritual state, neither of a stormy sea in the one nor of a prosperous voyage in the other. Between the two come Magelone's plaintive *Wie schnell verschwindet*, in which is a good example of the magical effect of Brahms's favourite sudden changes of harmony, Pierre's tenderly regretful *Muss es eine Trennung geben?* and the song for the Sultan's daughter, Sulima, which the master's admirers would probably agree in thinking the least successful of the fifteen. If it were conceivable that Brahms intended it to serve as a relief from the unflagging melodic beauty of the others, and as a preparation for the next one, it must be held to serve its purpose well. *Wie froh und frisch* is one of the songs which, with the splendid force of its figure of accompaniment and the swing of its melody, seems to bear the listener along towards the joyful ending of the story, as Pierre is borne by favouring breezes to his beloved Magelone. Kalbeck[1] thinks that the phrase set to the words, *In lieber, dämmernder Ferne*, are an intentional quotation from a military march peculiar to Hamburg, in which Brahms's father must often have taken part, and that it is used to express the composer's love of home, as though he came out of the character of Pierre for the moment. The final reunion of the lovers is celebrated in *Treue Liebe dauert lange*, in which there are several changes of theme and rhythm, the final *tempo primo* uniting them all into an epilogue of wonderful, if tranquil, impressiveness. It is no operatic finale, no limelit "apotheosis," but our hearts have been uplifted into a world of pure spiritual beauty in which we desire not to remember the gimcrack figures of make-believe chivalry.

We should possibly be justified in considering the twenty-five songs which were published in 1868, the year that saw the issue of the *Magelonelieder*, as being the *parerga*, the slighter, lyrical efforts, of the period during which were produced such important compositions as the quintet, Op. 34, the "Paganini" variations, the sextet in G, the pianoforte waltzes, and the horn trio, while the great *Requiem* was finished and published in that year. If there seem among the songs of this period to be a smaller proportion than usual of those which have been appropriated by the average concert-singer, and comparatively few that call for minute analysis, there are some at least which stand among the choicest specimens of their creator's work. The first and second of

[1] i. 457.

Op. 43, *Von ewiger Liebe* and *Die Mainacht*, *Sonntag*[1] from Op. 47, and *Wiegenlied* from Op. 49, for example, have probably few rivals in popular favour among the songs of Brahms, and they well deserve their position, for lovelier *genre* pictures do not exist in music. Each exactly expresses the mood of the words, and it is scarcely a mere coincidence that all are essentially characteristic of German peasant-life, excepting only *Mainacht*, which belongs to every class of life where love is known. An interesting discovery of the germ of the main climax-theme of *Von ewiger Liebe* was made by Kalbeck, in the single part-book of some compositions written for the Ladies' Choir at Hamburg. The melody set to the words, "Eisen und Stahl," etc., occurs in the part-book set to Uhland's *Brautgesang*—"Das Haus benedei' ich," etc., and is quoted by Kalbeck.[2] Two curious experiments in the simple accompaniment of what might be chorales are, *Ich schell' mein Horn in's Jammerthal* from Op. 43, and *Vergangen ist mir Glück und Heil* from Op. 48. The first appears again as the first of five male-voice choruses, Op. 41, and the second as the last of the seven choruses for mixed voices, Op. 62. As a whole set, Op. 46 is the most completely satisfactory, since *Die Kränze* is exquisitely tender, *Magyarisch* a fine example of restrained treatment of a possibly national

[1] Kalbeck (ii. 322) points out a very curious and most unfortunate misprint which has been repeated from the original edition of the song, in the collection of *Brahms-Texte*; the second stanza begins, in Uhland's *Volkslieder*, with the words, "So will mir doch die ganze Woche das Lachen nicht verjehn," which Kalbeck paraphrases as "Ich kann kein vergnügtes Gesicht mehr machen," or "I cannot allow myself to smile." In the printed song the last word appears as "vergehn," and so the meaning is turned into something like "I cannot help laughing," which is of course diametrically opposed to the meaning of the poet.

[2] i. 386.

though not very characteristic theme, *Die Schale der Vergessenheit* truly romantic (though the composer spoke of it as "wüst" or "dry"), and *An die Nachtigall* one of the most intimate and lovely of the composer's songs. *Botschaft* is the most important, and (with the exception of *Sonntag*) the most popular of Op. 47; its passion and spontaneity make it a worthy counterpart to *Meine Liebe ist grün. Liebesgluth* is not easy to perform or interpret adequately, but it is well worth study. *O liebliche Wangen* is built of such short phrases that it might seem trivial and even wearisome, were it not that in the second half of each verse (it is strophic in design) an effect of hurrying is produced by a different disposal of the quavers in the bar. *Der Gang zum Liebchen*, with which Op. 48 begins, is a German waltz of irresistible charm and swing; the short strophic songs which make up the bulk of the set are not of very great importance, but the last, *Herbstgefühl*, is deeply expressive and individual. *Am Sonntag Morgen*, the first of Op. 49, is an unforgettable picture of a peasant girl's disappointment, and a model of thematic development. We must suppose that *An ein Veilchen*, *Sehnsucht*, and *Abenddämmerung* have as yet come rarely to public performance because of the difficulty of their accompaniments, but when these are mastered, it is possible that the great beauty of the songs will be generally recognized, though they are hardly likely to win the rather unenviable popularity of the lovely *Wiegenlied*, of which no fewer than seventeen transcriptions of various kinds (eight for pianoforte alone!) are noted in Simrock's catalogue.[1]

Though only seven opus-numbers intervene in the

[1] As to the old tune used in accompaniment, see Kalbeck, i. 378.

list between these and the next group of songs, yet these opus-numbers represent compositions of such great import that we may expect a new stage of artistic growth to be reached after them. *Rinaldo* may not have taken a very high place among the composer's works, but the two string quartets, Op. 51, the *Liebeslieder*, the *Rhapsodie*, the *Schicksalslied*, and the *Triumphlied* were all published in the intermediate years, to say nothing of the orchestral variations on a theme of Haydn, which were actually issued after the songs we are now to consider. Opp. 57, 58, and 59, published in 1871–3, contain eight songs each, and there is little doubt that comparatively few amateurs know of them, because they were published by Rieter-Biedermann, a firm less often associated than that of Simrock with the works of Brahms. It is possible, too, that the opinion held by many people in Germany, that Daumer's words—to Op. 57—were too voluptuous for the family circle, may have had something to do with their neglect.[1] *Von waldbekränzter Höhe* is one of the songs which has the most direct appeal, and the recurring phrase, "Zurück, o Freund, zu dir, zu dir!" is set to one of the simply poignant musical phrases that Brahms knows how to use with such heart-stirring effect. *Wenn du mir zuweilen lächelst* is made a little difficult to interpret by the intrusion of a cross-rhythm that baffles ordinary performers; but it is no less beautiful in its intimate expression than *Es träumte mir, ich sei dir theuer*, or *Ach, wende diese Blick;* and indeed, to an audience already accustomed to the idioms of the composer, the whole set of Op. 57 might well be sung as a cycle. The seventh, *Die Schnur, die Perl' an Perle*, is a wonderful instance of economy of material, the theme

[1] See Kalbeck, ii. 372–3.

being used throughout with all kinds of half-playful modifications, but the deep and sincere emotion of the song being never lost sight of for a moment. The last, *Unbewegte laue Luft*, with its fine contrast between the still summer night and the passion in the lover's heart, might belong to the *Magelone* series, so warm yet so restrained is its expression, and so intimate its appeal. In *Blinde Kuh*, the first song of Op. 58, the harmonic progression gives exactly the feeling of the French word *désorienté;* one seems oneself to suffer from the blindfold player's uncertainty as to his bearings. *Während des Regens* may be a study for the *Regenlied* of the next set, but greater importance is here given to the actual dropping of the rain. In *Die Spröde*, which begins strophically and in light-hearted mood, the final verse turns off, in poetry and music, into a bitter upbraiding that is worthy of Heine. The exquisite *O komme, holde Sommernacht!* is one of those songs that seem to have been composed in a single inspiration, so fresh is the melody, so absolutely faithful the reflection of joyful expectancy, and so deft the handling of the beautiful figure of accompaniment. *In der Gasse* is remarkable, not only for its suggestion of a mood in which Schubert's *Doppelgänger* is supreme, but because the first notes of the voice-part give the figure that is mainly prominent in the accompaniment, though it is never sung again. *Vorüber* has many counterparts in the master's works, and it is not among his most individual things. The last of the set, *Serenade*, is the most effective for the public, and the guitar-figure of the opening is the best possible foil to the richly melodious voice-part and accompaniment of the middle section, where a deeper emotion is revealed. It is at least possible that this lovely song has escaped the attention of most singers, because of the similarity of its title to *Serenate* and *Ständchen*, both of which are elsewhere used by Brahms. *Dämm'rung senkte sich von oben*, the first of Op. 59, is as thoughtful as any of the set, but as landscape-painting in music it is less striking than the delicious barcarolle, *Auf dem See*, the final lines of which might serve as a motto for the whole of Brahms's songs: "Also spiegle du in Liedern was die Erde schönstes hat." The two rain-songs that follow, *Regenlied* and *Nachklang*, are virtually one song, for the thematic material is the same in both; we may fancy that the same shower suggests in the first no thought but of grateful coolness, while in the second it enhances the sorrow of a mourning heart. Musically, the gleam of sunshine in the second song is perhaps the most vivid passage, in its absolute faithfulness of delineation. But the system of economizing thematic material is here carried to a very high point; with the exception of a contrasting section in *Regenlied*, there is no note in voice-part or accompaniment of either song that does not derive from

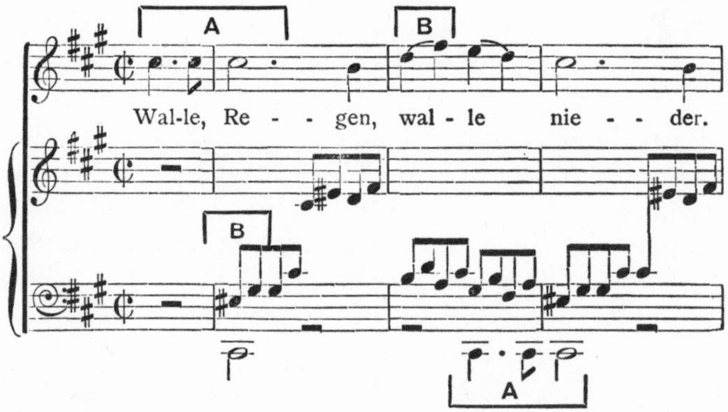

The use of the two component parts of the theme, here indicated by A and B, may be traced throughout the songs.

some part or other of the first phrase, and there is little cause for wonder that the composer liked the idea well enough to build upon the same material the finale of his first sonata for piano and violin, in G, Op. 78, published some years after these songs. Another setting of *Regenlied* was published, with a facsimile, by the Deutsche Brahms-Gesellschaft. The fifth of the series, *Agnes*, is a curious experiment in rhythm, following the suggestion of the words in its five-crotchet rhythm, and adding an extra "echo" bar of two crotchets to each alternate line, with rather bewildering effect. *Eine gute, gute Nacht* and *Dein blaues Auge* are tender songs in the Schumann manner; in *Mein wundes Herz* a feat of remarkable ingenuity is finely veiled beneath rare beauty of expression, and no one who is prejudiced against technical skill need notice that the accompaniment is identical with the vocal theme, but in notes of half the value. "Art is the veil of beauty over law," said Bishop Creighton, and the presence of mastery of handicraft surely does not mitigate against the spontaneity of the conception or the directness of the appeal. To many hearers, too, who are not contrapuntists enough to dissect the song, the feat itself may give pleasure quite without knowledge of the cause.

The set of nine songs which make up Op. 63 is less known than it ought to be, no doubt because the surpassing loveliness of one of the set has inevitably tended to overshadow the others. This, the famous *Meine Liebe ist grün*, which stands fifth in order, as the first of a pair called *Junge Lieder*, is one of the things concerning which it is impossible to guess how it came into the creator's brain. It is so ineffably spontaneous that it must seem to have been conceived in a single impulse and perfected at an instant. The glow of youthful passion has surely never been so superbly reflected in music, and the mind cannot grasp any process by which it was evolved, or think of any moment at which it was incomplete. Of the rest of the songs, *Frühlingstrost* has some of the same ardour, obtained by the interplay of combinations of triple time; *Erinnerung* is an exquisitely suave melody, built, like so many of Brahms's most attractive inventions, on the notes of a chord; if *An ein Bild* seems to have few of the qualities that make for effect in public, it is yet finely felt, and *An die Tauben* suggests the flight of a bird in its figure of accompaniment. The second of the *Junge Lieder* is scarcely a worthy companion for *Meine Liebe ist grün*, but in the little set called *Heimweh* is the tenderly plaintive *O wüsst' ich doch den Weg zurück*, in which the contrasting second theme is most deftly developed out of the first.

Four groups of songs, Opp. 69–72, precede the production of the second symphony, and many of them anticipate the lovely quality of that work. Op. 69 contains a large proportion of songs set to words apparently adopted from national sources, Bohemian or other. Almost all conform to the "volksthümlich" type, and the best known, the brilliant *Des Liebsten Schwur*, hardly departs from that pattern. The *Tambourliedchen* has a touch of realism in the words of the refrain, "blau, grau, blau," and the figure of accompaniment is obviously imitative. The last, *Mädchenfluch*, in which the girl turns all the curses into good wishes for her lover, is the kind of folk-ballad that must appeal to every one who understands the words. In the accompaniment to *Vom Strande* is the very roll of the sea. Though no national source is mentioned for *Ueber die See*, its purely strophic form and the simplicity of its structure proclaim it to have been suggested at least by folk-music. *Salome* is full of passion, and its effect seems to be attained by breaking the regularity of the rhythm in the second part. None of the four songs of Op. 70 are in the usual singer's repertory, though the plaintive directness of *Im Garten am Seegestade*, the ethereal rapture of *Lerchengesang*, the grace of *Serenate*, and the realism of *Abendregen* might have recommended them for practical use. Op. 71 begins with *Es liebt sich so lieblich im Lenze!* in a mood in which Brahms won greater renown later on; *An dem Mond* and *Geheimniss* are for the declared Brahms-lover rather than for the general public; but *Willst du, dass ich geh?* with its breathless longing and its masterly sense of passionate climax, cannot fail of its effect when adequately interpreted, and *Minnelied* is one of the most purely lovely inspirations to be found in music. In Op. 72 the first, *Alte Liebe*, is a piece of pure and characteristic Brahms; in *Sommerfäden* the gossamer threads are so faithfully portrayed in the accompaniment that one wants to break them away so as to see, as it were, the melody clear through the accompaniment, which gets the effect of thickness, though only two parts are used throughout. The *tessitura* of *O kühler Wald* makes it difficult to sing in almost any key, for the high voice required for the sustained close cannot give much effect to the notes at the beginning, which yet need to be fairly sonorous. In *Verzagen*, one of the most picturesque of all the master's songs, the breaking of waves on a sunless shore, with the backward wash of each as it retires, is wonderfully drawn in the accompaniment, and the sweeping melody is most striking. The last, a setting of Goethe's *Unüberwindlich*, is based on the theme of one of Domenico Scarlatti's harpsichord sonatas (the 31st of the edition of Ernst Pauer, and No. 214 in that of Alessandro Longo). Brahms has transposed it from D to A. It is a curious and powerful song, but never likely to be popular even with an educated public.

The five years between 1877, when all these songs saw the light, and 1883, when the next set was published, include among the compositions issued many of the most remarkable of Brahms's larger works. The second symphony, the two overtures, the first violin sonata, and the eight *Clavierstücke*, the violin concerto, and the second pianoforte concerto, to say nothing of *Nänie* and some motets, fill up the interval, and in these Brahms attained not merely to his full accomplishment, but to the full recognition of his contemporaries. Op. 75 are really more like songs in dialogue than duets, although, as they require two singers, they are most suitably analysed elsewhere. Op. 84 bears the strange inscription, "Für eine oder zwei Stimmen," but it is unlikely that on any occasion any of them have been sung by two persons. The modern singer, especially in Germany, is so anxious to show how many different sorts of voice-production he has learnt, that he misses no opportunity of singing songs in which two or more voices can be imitated. There is, indeed, an *ad libitum* part for the second voice simultaneously with the first, in the fifth of the set, *Spannung*, but here the music of each pair of stanzas is the same, and the male and female voices are supposed to alternate, as they are also in the best known of the set, *Vergebliches Ständchen*, though this is always sung by one singer, who must personify both the ardent lover and the disdainful lady at the window. Some of the set seem to be written with a view to allow the extremities of a voice of large compass to be displayed; the second, *Der Kranz*, has not a wide compass, but the *tessitura* of the daughter's part is soprano, that of the mother's, contralto. The contrasting moods of *Sommerabend* and of *In den Beeren*, in which the persons are again mother and daughter, are faithfully portrayed. A more tender and picturesque *Sommerabend* begins the set of six, Op. 85, and its tenderly expressive subject is carried on in the next, *Mondenschein*; the *Mädchenlied*, on a Servian motive in quintuple time, and the Bohemian *Ade!* belong to the "volksthümlich" class. *Frühlingslied* and *In Waldeinsamkeit* have been, quite intelligibly, overshadowed by others of Brahms's songs, for the second of the next set, *Feldeinsamkeit*, is warmly beloved wherever Brahms's name is known. Never was a more perfect picture of a summer noonday, in which the soul feels itself uplifted on the white clouds into the eternal spaces. The haunting beauty of *Therese* has hardly been sufficient to keep it in popular favour, for the average person likes to know a little more "what it is all about." Some very interesting passages about the shape of the melody in the opening bars are to be found in the *Herzogenberg Correspondence*, i. 180, 181 (trans., 157 ff.), showing how Brahms, even in his maturest period, was not above taking counsel with such friends as these. The swaying accompaniment of *Nachtwandler*, and the alternation of the major and minor harmonies, give strange atmospheric effect to the song, which, little known as it is, is yet one of the finest of the set. *Ueber die Haide* is remarkable for its economy of material, but for all that it is full of restrained energy. The broadly sweeping melody and accompaniment of *Versunken* make it effective when a singer and player are found to do it justice, though, as Frau von Herzogenberg said to the composer, the voice-part is too like "forked lightning" ("gewitterzackig").[1]

[1] *Correspondence*, i. 188; trans., 158.

Todessehnen, with its two movements, so nobly contrasted, carries our mind back to the *Magelone* songs, with which it may worthily be compared, for though it is even more earnest than they in its opening, its richly melodious second part is such as no one but Brahms could write. From this point in the songs of the master, every lyric is in the highest degree worthy of close attention, and while all the sets seem to cry aloud for continuous performance, there is not a single song in any of them which could be called ineffective by itself. The two beautiful songs for an alto voice with viola obbligato, Op. 91, usher in the period of the master's fullest maturity in his vocal work, for after the third symphony, Op. 90, his feeling for colour, and his unusual reticence in its use, must have been recognized on all hands. The *timbre* of the alto voice and that of the viola are so similar that the songs are like some beautiful drawing in very low tone; in the first, *Gestillte Sehnsucht*, the *obbligato* instrument and the voice seem to rival one another in the expression of a yearning desire, and in the second, *Geistliches Wiegenlied*, the theme of the old German Cradle-song of the Virgin is treated as a kind of *canto fermo* in the viola part, and as a piece of "colour" its figure illustrates the waving of the palms that shade the holy travellers. From Op. 94 to Op. 107 almost every song is of high importance, and the five for a deep voice that make up Op. 94 reveal to us a new Brahms to whom the graver aspects of life and destiny are dear. As a picture of middle age, and the shock of discovering that half one's life is over, was anything ever conceived more graphically than *Mit vierzig Jahren*? For one moment, after climbing the toilsome hill, we are on level ground; immediately we must descend, but with the descent comes peace and reconciliation with the inevitable. *Steig' auf*, *geliebte Schatten* invokes the departed spirit with such power that the call would seem irresistible.

The restless *Mein Herz ist schwer* leads finely into the noble *Sapphische Ode*, and the set is closed with a few wayward bars, *Kein Haus, keine Heimath*, from a play of Friedrich Halm. In *Sapphische Ode* the singers who are so fond of singing it may be warned that the last few bars of each verse, if performed in strict time, make the effect of a beautiful and well-ordered *rallentando*; if the time be slackened, over and above this, mere nonsense is the result. *Das Mädchen*, the first of Op. 95, also exists as a part-song, but it is more effective as a solo, and its rhythm of seven crotchets in a bar enables the capable singer to give an impression of spontaneous utterance. It is again from a Servian source, and is "volksthümlich" in the broadest sense. *Bei dir sind meine Gedanken* is exquisitely suave, and *Beim Abschied* is a remarkably successful example of the conflicting rhythm between three quavers in the voice part and four in the accompaniment; for a parallel to *Der Jäger* we must go back to the early *Schmied*, and this, as well as the next two, may have been suggested by a genuine folk-song. The Servian *Vorschneller Schwur* is a counterpart to many of the whimsical songs similarly labelled among Brahms's lyrics, and the Italian *Mädchenlied* is dainty, characteristic, and deeply expressive. In the last of the set, *Schön war, das ich dir weihte*, the strangely strong accent on the last syllable of "goldene" will startle purists in accentuation, but when the parallel phrase comes to balance the first strain, this is easily excused, and the song has rare charm. Two years after these, in 1886, appeared the four songs of Op. 96 and the six of Op. 97. The former set begins with the exquisitely poetical

Der Tod, das ist die kühle Nacht, and the lovely *Wir wandelten, wir zwei zusammen*, two songs which must always rank among the best of the master's works. The last-named turns a figure of single notes, off the regular beats of the bar, into a vivid picture of the chiming bells which the lover fancies he hears. After these eloquent songs, *Es schauen die Blumen?* and *Meerfahrt* seem a little wanting in spontaneity, but the last is sincerely plaintive.[1]

Two bird-songs begin Op. 97, the tender threnody of *Nachtigall* and the fluttering movement of *Auf dem Schiffe;* the others of the set are "volksthümlich"; the vivid *Entführung* is actually strophic, with the exception of an intercalated bar at the end, put in in deference to Frau von Herzogenberg's opinion;[2] and *Komm' bald* is so studiedly simple that it might well be a folk-song. The words of *Dort in den Weiden* come from the lower Rhine, those of *Trennung* from Suabia. This last is another instance of alteration made at the suggestion of Frau von Herzogenberg.[3]

In 1889 there came out fifteen songs, Opp. 105, 106, and 107, containing a wonderful proportion of masterpieces. The first of these sets, five songs for a low voice, might be taken as representing in fullest perfection the art of Brahms as a song-writer in all its aspects. The fourth symphony, the double concerto, and the second sonata for violoncello and piano, which almost immediately preceded them, belong to the most intimate of the master's compositions, and it is not surprising to find that some of the songs belong to the same category, but the long-drawn

[1] See the *Herzogenberg Correspondence*, ii. 61, 62; trans., 227.

[2] *Ibid.*, ii. 65; trans., 230.

[3] *Ibid.*, ii. 64; trans., 229, 230.

sweetness of the violin sonata in A, Op. 100 (second theme of the first movement), finds a counterpart in the first song of Op. 105, *Wie Melodien zieht es* (the song was written first), while the peasant-energy of the *Zigeunerlieder* for vocal quartet, Op. 103, appears in some measure in the lower Rhenish *Klage*, and still more in the intensely dramatic *Verrath.* The remaining two songs of the set show us Brahms in his most individual moods, and it is not easy to point to any single songs, of whatever date or country, that are worthy to be mentioned in the same breath with *Immer leiser* and *Auf dem Kirchhofe.*[1] *Immer leiser* lays open to us the inmost depths of a devoted woman's love, and the tenderness of the quiet melody reaches a point of irresistible pathos at the words—

"Oft im Traume hör' ich dich
Rufen draus vor meiner Thür,"

while the passionate close of the song marks a height that even Brahms has seldom touched elsewhere. It is strange that a subtle and sensitive woman like Frau von Herzogenberg should have objected at first to the succession of chords of the $\frac{6}{4}$ in the last verse, which so exactly paint the dying woman's longing in all its weak intensity.[2] *Auf dem Kirchhofe* touches a chord of emotion that was always very dear to Brahms, but never more so than in his later years. Mortality, the physical horrors of the grave, the dreary passage of the soul from earth, form one side of the picture; and though the composer's religion was essentially undogmatic, yet he allows himself to hold

[1] There is an allusion to this song in the finale of the violin sonata in A major, Op. 100, written after it.

[2] See the *Correspondence*, ii. 132, 135 ff. ; trans., 291, 293.

out hope for the future life; and as in the *Schicksalslied* and the *Requiem*, so here, the contrast of the two moods is full of spiritual suggestion.

If Op. 106 contains nothing quite as great as these two, it must not be forgotten that it begins with the delightfully genial *Ständchen*, and contains, in *Ein Wanderer*, one of the most deeply poetical of all the songs.[1] This and *Es hing ein Reif* seem to belong to the same class as Schubert's *Winterreise*, but the former at least is on an even higher plane of imagination. In *Auf dem See* there is a charming barcarolle-measure together with thoroughly Brahmsian harmonies, and in *Meine Lieder* the figure of accompaniment, an inverted arpeggio, gives an unmistakable foreshadowing of one of the latest pianoforte solos, Op. 119, No. 1. Op. 107 consists of songs in a lighter mood, for *An die Stolze* is half in play, *Der Salamander* is wholly humorous, *Das Mädchen spricht* exquisitely graceful in its vocal outline, *Maienkätzchen* a "volksthümliches Lied" of the prettiest sort imaginable, and *Mädchenlied* a lovely little sad song in popular style.

It would scarcely be a profitable task to subject each one of the forty-nine *Deutsche Volkslieder* which came out in 1894 to the same detailed analysis as has been given to the other songs; but these arrangements of German folk-songs are a model for every one who cares for national music. The usual plan is that two sets of harmonies are given for each song, to be used with alternate stanzas; sometimes, where the mood of the song requires it, there is a third harmonization; but in all cases the natural character of the tune has always suggested the style of the

[1] As to the order of composition of this and *Nachtigall*, Op. 97, No. 1, see *Herzogenberg Correspondence*, ii. 63; trans., 225 ff.

accompaniment, and there is throughout the collection no example of the tortured harmonies we so often hear in folk-song arrangements, which suggest that the arranger has been anxious to show how clever he is. Such things as *Die Sonne scheint nicht mehr* and *Maria ging aus wandern* show how richly developed is this type of folk-song in Germany; *Schwesterlein* is a poignant drama in miniature; *Mein Mädel hat einen Rosenmund* is deliciously mischievous; and *Es steht ein Lind'* and *In stiller Nacht* are exquisite things which have never been so beautifully set. The latter also occurs as a part-song in the choral *Deutsche Volkslieder*, which appeared in 1864. The last of the seven books of the later collection consists of songs in which the "Vorsänger" is supported by a small choir, and, as though to round off the work of his life, Brahms gives, as the last of the set, *Verstohlen geht der Mond*, which served as the slow movement of his piano sonata in C, Op. 1.

It remains to speak of the work which set the crown on the master's achievement both as a song-writer and a profound religious thinker, the *Vier ernste Gesänge*, Op. 121, the last composition published during his lifetime. They were inspired by the illness and death of Frau Schumann, as appears from Litzmann's *Life*, iii. 609.

Throughout his life, the creeds of the Churches had little appeal for him, and dogma must have been repugnant to him always. But his contemplation of the "four last things" bore manifold fruit, not only in the *Requiem*, but in various choral works, which must be discussed later. As early as the *Schicksalslied* he realized the importance of a hope of life beyond the grave, a hope which, however vague, was yet sure.

There, it is true, this hope is only expressed instrumentally, in the beautiful orchestral epilogue to Hölderlin's despondent poem, an epilogue which raises our thoughts to the serenity with which it began. In the *Requiem* he leads our thoughts step by step from considering the state of the happy dead to the idea of consolation, and finally to the Beatific Vision of rapturous praise. In these four "serious songs," as they are called in English, we begin with the reflection that as death is common to man and beast alike, so there is no assurance of a difference in the future state between one and the other. The rapid passages in the accompaniment seem to suggest that animal life ceases like the dust on the highway. The next song seems to say, "Even if there be no future life, the dead in their perfect unconsciousness are to be envied, rather than the living who must see around them trouble and sorrow they cannot relieve." The same idea leads, in the third song, to the praise of death when it comes to the poor and afflicted; and this is in some ways the most beautiful of the four, as its picture of deep sympathy with the oppressed and its musical contrasts between the aspects of death to the rich and to the poor make it most impressive. With the last of the four songs we change from the gloom and uncertainty of the hope of immortality held out in the Old Testament and Apocrypha to the Christian conviction, and to the love that spreads abroad to all mankind as the result of that conviction. In strongest contrast with the words of Ecclesiastes and Ecclesiasticus, the abstract of the Pauline description of "charity" in 1 Cor. xiii. comes with wonderful life, vigour, and confidence. The passage "Wir sehen jetzt durch einen Spiegel," which represents, no doubt, Brahms's own feeling of indefinite hope, has a serenity as of a beautiful sunset, and it is difficult to imagine a happier ending to a glorious creative career than this song[1] or the posthumous chorale-prelude which possibly was composed later, *O Welt, ich muss dich lassen.*

The last set of songs has the great advantage of an English translation (by Paul England), which echoes the Scriptural words with remarkable faithfulness and yet suits the music to perfection. The less said the better about the translation of the great majority of the other songs, although objectors were assured that they were "the only translation authorized by the composer." They fulfil few, if any, of the ideals of words for music; they frequently make nonsense, or contradict the inflection of the voice part, and are seldom even tolerable in effect. There are exceptional cases in which the translations are quite good; those of the "Magelonelieder," by Andrew Lang and R. H. Benson, many of the "unauthorized" versions of Lady Macfarren, Paul England, Claude Aveling, and others, and, perhaps best of all, an anonymous collection (privately printed) of *Songs translated from the German* containing admirable versions of ten of the songs, and four of the "Volkslieder." It is not impossible, of course that the atrocious style of the "authorized" translations by forcing singers to use the original words, have done good work in endearing the German poems to the British public.

[1] See the *Joachim Correspondence*, ii. 287, 288.

CHAPTER VIII

MUSIC FOR SOLO VOICES IN COMBINATION

AS a complement to the songs for one voice, the far smaller group of works for vocal ensemble must next be considered. It begins with Op. 20, three duets for soprano and contralto, the first of which, *Die Meere*, recalls the duets of Mendelssohn in its gentle suavity. The other two, *Weg der Liebe*, are on the theme, "Love will find out the way," and the energy and spirit of the first finds a noble counterpart in the calmly confident mood of the second. It is not, however, until Op. 28, four duets for alto and baritone, that the real Brahms is to be perceived. They are dedicated to Frau Amalie Joachim, and were published in 1864; the first, *Die Nonne und der Reiter*, is poignantly expressive, the second, *Vor der Thür*, deals with Brahms's favourite topic of an ardent lover vainly trying to make his lady admit him to her bower, and is naturally the most popular of the set. *Es rauschet das Wasser* has a changing rhythm which is so handled that it is felt to flow on from beginning to end quite continuously. It is full of conviction, grace, and energy. In the last, *Der Jäger und sein Liebchen* are of two different temperaments, and utter their various desires above a beautifully maintained figure of accompaniment.

The same idea of different temperaments inspired the

first of the vocal quartets, Op. 31, *Wechsellied zum Tanze,* set to Goethe's words. The measure is that of a minuet, and the one pair of "indifferent" dancers, thinking only of the joys of the dance, is identified with the main theme, while the "tender" pair, who only think of love, come forward at the trio-portion, all four joining in the elaborate coda. There is a kind of foreshadowing of the *Liebeslieder* in this charming piece, which is too rarely to be heard. The second, *Neckereien*, is another dialogue between the two men representing the lover and the two women as the beloved, the four uniting their voices at the end. The use of rapid triplets at this point is vividly picturesque. *Der Gang zum Liebchen* is on the lovely theme that the composer used for the first time in one of his waltzes, Op. 39 (written before the vocal quartets, though published after them). Its words were used again in the song of the same name, Op. 48, No. 1.

It may be noticed that up to Op. 28 the concerted vocal music is entirely on dialogue-motives with the single exception of this last quartet, where the four voices are used after the simplest pattern of a part-song. This purely lyrical use of solo voices, without any hint of personality, is one of the things that make the *Liebeslieder-Walzer* (Op. 52) so full of charm; and a good deal of that charm is lost if singers insist on putting vocal "colour" or individuality into music that was never meant to have these qualities; for the voices are to be subordinated to the four-hand pianoforte part throughout, and the players should arrange their own readings of the waltzes, not so as to suit the singers' convenience, but quite independently.[1] The quartets are "ländler" rather than waltzes, but their

[1] On the question of this subordination, and in connexion with the wording of the title-page, Max Kalbeck's *Life* (ii. pp. 292–6) may be consulted.

entrain is not to be withstood by any hearer if the proportion between players and singers is kept, and if the voices blend well together. A curious instance of the proportion required is in the soprano (or alto) solo, No. 7, where the "primo" of the pianists has to play the melody in unison with the voice; the instrumental part has far more marks of expression than the vocal, and at the end it actually has a prominent turn, while the singer is required to make what must seem to her an ineffective end. No. 6, in which the tenor is the prominent part, *Ein kleiner, hübscher Vogel*, and No. 9, *Am Donaustrande*, where the alto leads, will always be the favourite portions of the work, but the animation of *Nein, es ist nicht auszukommen*, No. 11, and the succeeding *Schlosser, auf!* must appeal to those for whom without them the sweetness of the tunes might have an almost cloying effect. But the peculiarity of the *Liebeslieder* is not so much in the beauty of its single numbers as in the curious and completely successful treatment of a "colour" that is quite new to music, the subdued voices sustaining the harmonic scheme, like some exquisite wind instrument, while the rhythm and sparkle of the ländler-measure is kept up by the piano. No further proof of Brahms's power as a colourist, when he chose to exert it, could be required than these quartets.

Although out of their proper order, it will be convenient to consider next the *Neue Liebeslieder*, a second set of similar pieces, which appeared in 1875 as Op. 65, six years after the first set. As compared with those, they strike us as more austere and even gloomy in their expression, though the words of these, like those of the others, are taken from Daumer's *Polydora*. Such dark and splendid things as *Finstere Schatten der Nacht*, *Ihr schwarzen Augen*, *Schwarzer Wald*, and *Flammenauge* are even richer in colour than the quartets of the first set and the greater proportion of solo numbers gives the individual voices slightly more prominence, besides which the subordination of the singers to the players is not insisted on by the master as it was in the first set, where the title stands as "für Pianoforte zu vier Händen (und Gesang *ad libitum*)"; the words "für vier Singstimmen und Pianoforte zu vier Händen" suggest that the pianoforte part is relatively of less importance in the second set than in the first. The most enchanting feature of the whole is the epilogue (Goethe's words), *Nun, ihr Musen, genug!* in which the slow ländler-movement is expanded into a grave measure of $\frac{9}{8}$, the faint suggestion of the dance-rhythm being allowed to die away gradually upon the ear.

To resume the chronological order: the four duets, Op. 61, are for soprano and contralto, and begin with the well-known *Die Schwestern*, the light mood of which seems to prophesy tears to come; *Klosterfräulein* is a picture of regret that almost reaches despair; but *Phänomen* is one of the loveliest inspirations of the master's middle period; it seems, like *Minnelied* or *Meine Liebe ist grün*, to have come into being at a moment with a single impulse of creation. The fourth, *Die Boten der Liebe*, is one of those soaring compositions that suggest the swift, steady flight of a bird. In all these duets the parts move together, and there is no suggestion of a dialogue between two persons.

Op. 64 consists of three exceedingly beautiful quartets, which are far too little known, since they are most vocal and grateful to the singers, as well as really effective. *An die Heimath* opens with richly disposed harmonies, and a triplet figure treated in free canon suggests the power with which the thought of home draws the heart. At the words "freundliche Heimath" a phrase is started by the tenor voice, and imitated by the rest, which is eloquent of longing for peace, and the little unaccompanied passages which follow it, together with the concise development, carry out the same idea. It is one of the most elaborate of the compositions for concerted solo voices, the following quartet, *Der Abend*, being only second to it in this respect; both are compositions of flowing beauty and unity. The third, *Fragen*, is a curious dialogue between the tenor, who personifies the heart of a lover, and the rest of the quartet, who utter the questions that may be supposed indicative of his mental and other qualities. It is carried on with humour and pathos combined, and where a quartet-party has a first-rate tenor it is always effective.

The five duets for soprano and contralto, Op. 66, are again for the most part homophonic. The first two, *Klänge* (1 and 2), are full of pathetic expression, and the second is built on the theme that appeared in the slow movement of the F sharp minor sonata, Op. 2. The third, *Am Strande*, with a wonderful modulation in the middle, is one of the most "intimate" of Brahms's duets; *Jägerlied*, the only one of this set in dialogue, passes from an almost coquettish mood into deep despair at the close. *Hüt' du dich* is a simple "volksthümlich" setting of the words that are familiar to English-speaking people in Longfellow's version, *I know a maiden fair to see.*

Op. 75 consists entirely of dialogues, and the set is nearly akin to the songs "for one or two voices," Op. 84, which were discussed in the last chapter (see p. 179). The first, *Edward*, for alto and tenor, is on the subject of the same folk-song that impressed Brahms so much at the time of the pianoforte *Balladen*, Op. 10; it comes from Herder's collection of "Volkslieder," and is, of course,

Scottish in origin. To trace back the history of the ballad, through the various "Lord Rendal," "Lord Ronald," and "King Henry" stages, is beyond our present purpose; but it may be said that we seem to have a faint recollection of the suspected murder of Henry I or II of England.[1]

More important to the musician is the treatment of the successive repetitions of the word "O" at the end of each line of the poem. Like Loewe, Brahms has varied its expression until it finally becomes a dying cry. To make it pregnant with dramatic meaning is perhaps of doubtful legitimacy, but the result is very striking. It was of course originally intended as a meaningless extension of the line, just as "ah" or "sir" was often put into the refrain of rustic songs. William Webbe, in *A Discourse of English Poetrie* (1586), refers to the "ryming ballet-mongers who put in an 'a' to make a jercke in the end." Brahms's mistake in giving significance to what was originally an unmeaning adjunct to the line is surely pardonable enough. The second of the duets, *Guter Rath*, is sung by a mother and daughter, the latter of whom has it all her own way at the end. *So lass uns wandern*, for soprano and tenor, has a short section for the two voices together, and is very fluent and expressive; the last of the set, *Walpurgisnacht*, is for two sopranos, and, excepting for two notes in which both voices are heard at once, might be sung by one singer with a gift for sudden changes of vocal colour, such as is required for the songs, Op. 84.

The four quartets, Op. 92, begin with *O schöne Nacht*, the opening bars of which, with the piano arpeggios and the richly harmonized phrase, are extraordinarily full of "atmosphere." It is a worthy companion to *An die Heimath*. *Spätherbst* begins as if the lower voices were

[1] See *Folk-Song Society's Journal*, iii. 43.

going to keep up an accompaniment to the soprano, but after four bars they take a more prominent part and are interwoven with great beauty of effect. *Abendlied* gives the picture of a troubled heart gradually receiving comfort from the peace of evening, and the two little unaccompanied cadences near the end are of incomparable charm. The two sections of *Warum* are finely contrasted, but the quartet is not one of the master's most successful pieces of vocal ensemble.

The *Zigeunerlieder*, Op. 103, are eleven in number, and eight of them were arranged for a single voice by the composer; they are not really very effective in the form of solos, although they have been more often performed in this way than according to the master's original plan. As quartets, they are most exciting, and the changes of colour, from the single voice of the "Vorsänger" to the ensemble of the quartet, and the imitations of the gipsy "Cimbalom" on the piano, make them of the widest possible appeal. The third, *Wisst ihr, wann mein Kindchen*, is almost a csárdás in structure, a sedate allegretto being succeeded by a spirited allegro.

In Op. 112, the master's last set of quartets, he added four more to the number of *Zigeunerlieder*, and the new are at least as fine as any in the first set. *Rothe Rosenknospen* has infinite charm, and its ending is of special beauty. The fourth, too, *Liebe Schwalbe*, has the genuine gipsy atmosphere, and all belong to the music of outdoor life. The two quartets by which these are preceded in the collection are a plaintive and haunting *Sehnsucht* and *Nächtens*, one of Brahms's rare experiments in unusual times, a five-crotchet rhythm being maintained throughout.

CHAPTER IX

THE CHORAL WORKS

THE first choral works of Brahms are more experimental, more tentative, than his first essays in the other forms. A Mass in canon and some other vocal canons are referred to in the letters to Joachim as early as 1856, but they were not published.[1] If we compare the gentle, suave *Ave Maria* for female voices with orchestral (or organ) accompaniment (Op. 12) with the passionate *Liebestreu*, the first three piano sonatas, the trio, Op. 8, or the serenade in D, we shall be struck with the timid and almost conventional style which it exhibits. It is charmingly flowing in a pastoral manner, and to the student of the master's works it has an interest, in that it foreshadows some of the qualities of the chorus "How lovely is Thy dwelling-place" in the *Requiem*. Is it a mere coincidence, or from some unconsciously received suggestion in the music itself, that in the most easily accessible edition of the piece, in Novello's series of anthems, it is set to the words, "Blessed are they that dwell in Thy house"? At the same time with this, in the year 1861, was published the companion work, *Begräbnissgesang*, Op. 13, a funeral march for six-part chorus, accompanied by wind instruments (without flutes or trumpets, but with trom-

[1] See *Joachim Correspondence*, i. 136, 147–9; and Kalbeck, i. 277.

BRAHMS CONDUCTING

FROM A DRAWING BY PROF. VON BECKERATH

bones). As Mr. Colles has said, "Though there is no thematic likeness, it has something of the solemn tread more fully exemplified in the great funeral march of the *Deutsches Requiem*." But there is another and more curious foreshadowing of a well-known piece of music, and the circumstances entirely preclude the idea that the author of the later piece can have known Brahms's early chorus; the impression of a hollow vault plunged in gloom, which is created by the vocal and orchestral colouring employed, is exactly the same as that which makes it impossible to forget the scene of the procession of Titurel's body in the third act of *Parsifal*. As Wagner was not sufficiently tolerant of the music of Brahms to investigate his early works, which were probably not as easily accessible in Germany as they are now, and as there is no recorded performance of the *Begräbnissgesang* at any time or place where Wagner could have been present the circumstance is of course nothing but the merest coincidence.

Another experiment, this time a very beautiful one, is the set of four part-songs for three-part female choir with accompaniment of two horns and harp, Op. 17. Never were there more romantic effects of instrumental colouring than are to be found in all the songs, the first of which, *Es tönt ein voller Harfenklang*, opens with a horn-signal that is a worthy companion to certain passages in which similar sounds are made with romantic intention, such as the famous passage in the finale of Chopin's pianoforte concerto in F minor, the opening of the second act of *Tristan*, and the introduction to the finale of Brahms's own first symphony in C minor. It might be thought that to accompany all four songs, of such very different character, with the same instruments must be a mistake, but nothing can be more varied than the treatment of the instruments throughout; and in the Clown's song from *Twelfth Night*, "Come away, come away, Death," the light horn notes and the staccato chords of the harp just give the touch of the whimsical that the song needs. The third, a setting of Eichendorff's *Gärtner*, is almost Mendelssohnian in its suavity, and as a purely lyrical utterance it comes in well among the others. The last, *Gesang aus Fingal*, to Ossianic words, is exquisitely pathetic, and in the latter part, where the chorus is divided into four parts,[1] there is an unaccompanied passage, and the difficulty of making simple homophonic writing sound interesting is satisfactorily solved. The unisonous chromatic passage in which the howling of Trenar's dogs is referred to is joined in by the horn with weird effect, and the elegiac force of the whole culminates in a fine climax, in which the harp is prominently used.

The first experiment in writing for voices unaccompanied throughout was made in the set of seven *Marienlieder*, for four-part choir. They are part-songs of the utmost simplicity, in all of which the melody of the top part is prominent, although in all there are points of imitation, and the first, *Der englische Gruss*, ends with a little canonic passage. *Maria's Kirchgang* uses the bass part only in one of the seven verses, and when it comes in the chiming of the bells is imitated. All the other verses are identical in their music. *Maria's Wallfahrt* is on the same words as the *Volkslied* in the second book of Brahms's collection, and it is curious to see the points of resemblance and difference between the two, for the part-song is not actually founded on the traditional melody.

[1] This is surely enough to prove that the ordinary English title of the songs, "trios," is inapplicable, and that they are only meant for choral use.

The quaint *Jäger*, in which the Angel of the Annunciation is represented as blowing his horn, is one of the most effective of the songs, and *Ruf zur Maria* the most deeply expressive. The quiet motion of the inner parts in this and in *Magdalena* is a sign that the composer's technique in choral writing was growing in skill and certainty. The last, *Maria's Lob*, alters its time at the fourth bar of each verse in a manner that reminds us of the "ballets" of the Italian and English composers of the Elizabethan times.

In the setting of Psalm xiii for female voices with organ accompaniment, Op. 27, we find a strange disregard of the physical limitations of the human voice, for the *tessitura* of the first soprano part is incredibly bad, the high notes being unrelieved for many bars together; many singers would rather sing the choral part of the Ninth Symphony than this short psalm, which for the rest has fewer points of interest than are generally found in Brahms.

In Op. 29, two motets for five-part choir unaccompanied, Brahms deliberately adopts the style of Bach in his "chorale-choruses"; the first, on the chorale, *Es ist das Heil uns kommen her*, presents the melody in crotchets over moving quavers in the lower parts, and the five-part fugue which follows it treats each line of the melody separately, the line itself being given out by the first basses, and fugally treated by the rest. The sonorous five-part opening of the second motet, *Schaffe in mir, Gott*, is followed by a four-part fugue of the utmost strictness, which taxes the powers of even the most cultivated choirs to sing without losing pitch. A new movement starts with a beautiful passage for the three male voices, *Tröste mich wieder*, answered by the female singers, this time increased to three parts of their own; another four-part fugal section, *Und der freudige Geist*, makes a brilliant ending to the motet, or cantata, as it might almost be called. In these motets the study of Bach's methods completed Brahms's technical education, and the mastery he had now acquired was shown again in a setting of a *Geistliches Lied*, by Paul Flemming, Op. 30, in which the chorale-melody of *Herr Jesu Christ, du höchstes Gut* is treated after the manner of Bach, each line set separately with organ interludes, with a finely flowing figure between them, and the final "Amen" is of singular beauty and impressiveness. The voices are treated canonically, the tenor imitating the soprano, and the bass the alto, at the ninth below.

In the same year, 1864, was published a set of fourteen *Deutsche Volkslieder* without opus-number. They are dedicated to the Vienna Singakademie, and while studiedly simple in design are no less masterly in treatment than the more elaborate motets just mentioned. *Von edler Art* is perhaps the loveliest of the first book; it has a hint of the madrigalian style about it, as has also No. 5, *Täublein weiss.* A very quaint little piece is that in honour of the *Heilige Märtyrer Emmerano*, a bishop of Ratisbon. The second book begins with the exquisite *In stiller Nacht*, which was afterwards arranged for one voice, among the *Volkslieder* published in Brahms's later life. In its choral arrangement it seems more effective and more solemn. The last, *Der englische Jäger*, is more or less madrigalian in style, but whether imitative or not all these little pieces show a great advance on the earlier works for choir alone.

In Op. 37, three *Geistliche Chöre* for female voices unaccompanied, we find the companion pieces to those, Opp. 12, 17, 44, which were written for the Hamburg Ladies' Choir; these three were published in 1866. *O bone Jesu* is short and reverent, and although the progressions in the first bar would shock the student of old ecclesiastical music, yet all three of the choruses suggest the masters of the past, and if the *Adoramus* breathes of Palestrina, the third, *Regina Coeli*, reminds us of Morley's two-part canzonets, for the two soloists carry on the greater part of the piece, the choir interjecting "Alleluja" here and there.

The male part-songs, Op. 41, begin with the solemn *Ich schwing' mein Horn;* the second, *Freiwillige her!* starts with a phrase that is difficult in time till the natural accentuation of the words is considered, and then it is obviously the only proper way in which they could be set. This and the rest of the set are clearly intended for military use, and this one has a startling and very beautiful change at the close from E flat to C major. *Geleit* is supposed to be sung at a soldier's funeral, and *Marschiren*, with its amusing words about the tedium of barrack life, is so simple in design that one almost wonders why it was not taken as a national song in the Franco-German War. The last, *Gebt Acht!* is enough to explain the result of that war; one feels that the nation which could produce so noble and direct an utterance was sure to win. But when these songs were published, in 1867, there was no immediate anticipation of the war. The next published composition, three six-part songs unaccompanied, Op. 42, contains one of the best known of Brahms's choral pieces, the lovely *Vineta*, with its fine vocal colouring that gives the exact atmospheric effect of looking down through clear water to depths in which a city lies buried. The first of the three *Abendständchen* has the female voices singing in antiphony to the male, and a curious descending cadence, in which the major and minor modes play, as it were, into each other's hands. The third, *Darthula's Grabgesang*, is the longest of the three, and is partly in dialogue, the two contralto voices and the three male parts being in antiphony at first, and afterwards the soprano, two altos, and tenor are answered by the two basses. This treatment enhances the effect of the great ensemble when it does come, at the words, "Wach auf, wach auf, Darthula!" There is a most pathetic end at "Sie schläft." Though published in the year of the three *Geistliche Chöre* for female voices, the twelve *Lieder und Romanzen* for the same combination are numbered Op. 44 in the list. They begin with *Dem holdseligen sonder Wank*, with a delicious effect of out-of-the-way rhythm; *Der Bräutigam*, *Fragen*, and the four *Lieder aus dem Jungbrunnen* are all in the rather conventional style of the ordinary German part-songs; the barcarole, *Fidelin*, has far more character, and *Die Nonne* is very fine, its final phrase being of exquisite pathos. *Die Braut* has a curious rhythmic effect; it is in $\frac{3}{2}$ time, and after two bars, the crotchets going on regularly, the time changes to $\frac{4}{4}$, so that two crotchet rests seem always to be superfluous. The last, *Märznacht*, has beautifully treated chromatic voice parts above an arpeggio accompaniment; for though the words "a capella" appear in the title, there is an *ad libitum* pianoforte accompaniment, though it is so light that a very small choir is needed if the accompaniment is used.

With such studies, as they may be called, did Brahms prepare himself for the execution of the scheme which occupied him, though not continuously, for some five years. It is unnecessary here to pursue the inquiry into the original object of the *Deutsches Requiem*, Op. 45, and to discuss whether the subject was originally suggested to Brahms by the death of Schumann or not (see pp. 23, 24).

What concerns us more nearly in approaching the

work for the purposes of analysis, is that its first three numbers were presented to the public of Vienna at one of the Gesellschaft's concerts, 1 December, 1867; that on Good Friday, 1868 (10 April), it was given as then completed in the cathedral of Bremen, under the direction of the composer, Reinthaler having organized the performance and conducting the rest of the concert. The work was not finally enriched with the present No. 5, the soprano solo with chorus, until after the second performance by the "Union," conducted by Reinthaler, on 27 April at Bremen.[1] This last touch was put to the work in May, 1868, and in February, 1869, the completed *Requiem* was given in the Gewandhaus at Leipzig. Those who are fond of making facts fit in with their preconceived ideas have professed to trace a lack of unity in the work which took so long to reach completion; but in truth the more deeply it is studied the more unity it seems to possess. Of course its plan has nothing in common with the Requiem Mass of the Catholic Church, and so far the use of the word "requiem" is perhaps rather forced, since there is no hint of prayer offered on behalf of the dead. The blessing pronounced by Christ on those who mourn, and the blessing of the Holy Spirit on the faithful departed uttered in the Revelation of St. John, make the beginning and the end of the scheme similar in conception, and the same musical theme is used at the end of both the first and last choruses, the chief difference being that in the last violins are employed, while in the opening number of the work a specially sombre colour is imparted to the orchestration by their absence. The words which might be inscribed over the *Requiem*, and over every one of its sections—"Sorrow shall be turned to joy"—have guided the master

[1] See the *Correspondence with Reinthaler* (Brfwchsl. iii.), 1–23.

even in this slight detail. How closely considered was the choice of words may be realized in the *Correspondence with Reinthaler* (pp. 7–11), where the composer gives his reasons for not making the words more definitely and explicitly Christian. The first number consoles those who mourn the death of a beloved one; the second begins with the wonderful death-march of the race on its way to the grave, and places in opposition to the brevity of human life the fact that "the Lord's word endureth for ever." As these words are uttered, the voices break out with the jubilant words, "The redeemed of the Lord shall return and come to Zion with songs and everlasting joy upon their heads." In the third number we start again from the level of human sorrow and anxiety, with the baritone solo, "Lord, make me to know the measure of my days," as though the universal fate were forgotten in the individual desire to peer into the future. Everything breathes of uncertainty and impatience, and the wonderful passage in which these culminate, "Now, Lord, what do I wait for?" leads to the true solution, "My hope is in Thee," the notes of which grow from the bass part through the others in succession, up to the famous pedal fugue, "But the righteous souls are in the hand of God," where the persistent bass note, D (which was a dreadful stumbling-block to the first hearers), lays the foundation of a confidence that is not to be shaken. This is something more than mere tone-painting, for the unchanging bass cannot fail to convey the feeling of steadfastness that the words contain; there is in the former number, at the words, "the early and latter rain," a use of staccato notes on the violins which might be interpreted as a touch of realism, but whether it is so or not, here at all events the music illustrates a spiritual truth. The middle number of the work for once does not open sorrowfully, but leads us on from the conviction that the dead are in God's hands to the contemplation of the calm celestial joys. The human longing "for the courts of the Lord" is indeed expressed, by one voice after another, in its middle section, but the prevailing note is one of peaceful happiness.

The next part (added last of all, after the Bremen performance) contains the utterances of the departed spirit in the soaring, sustained notes of the soprano solo, with occasional interjections in the chorus, whose words, "As one whom his own mother comforteth," point to the circumstance that was in the composer's mind when he wrote it.[1] The words, "Ye shall again behold me," are set to the same notes as the opening figure of accompaniment, and they are echoed in notes of double the length in the choral "Yea, I will comfort you." In the next section we reach the greatest climax of the work; the chorus begins, "Here on earth have we no continuing place," and although by this time the uncertainty is not hopeless, yet the faint hopes kindled by what has gone before need the confirmation of the words, "Lo, I unfold unto you a mystery," uttered by the baritone solo, and leading to the marvellously vivid description of the change that is to come to pass "at the sound of the trumpet." The section, "For the trumpet shall sound," in rapid triple time, corresponds in some measure to the *Dies irae* of the Catholic requiems, but as Death is swallowed up in victory, so the tumult of this choral passage is merged into the magnificent fugal ending, "Worthy art Thou to be praised." This climax is musically one of the most ardent and uplifting things in the whole range of music,

[1] See the *Joachim Correspondence*, ii. 51, etc., for certain details which the composer altered in deference to Joachim's opinion.

and forms the real ending of the work. It must have seemed an impossible task to write anything to follow this without making a terrible anticlimax, and yet it is obvious that the note of rapture with which this chorus ends must not dominate a composition called a "requiem." The epilogue, "Blessed are the dead," seems the only possible close to the whole, so right and so restful is its mood. The long cantabile passage, first for sopranos and then for basses, with the swaying accompaniment of strings, prepares us for the solemn declaration, "Yea, saith the Spirit, for they rest from their labours," in which the soprano voices are silent, and the horns and trombones are used alone for the accompaniment. One of the most subtle effects in the work is the resumption of the theme of the opening chorus at the close; for the mood of the closing chorus is made to assimilate itself gradually to that of the opening, so that the transition is made almost imperceptibly. A kindred piece of refinement is at the end of the string quartet in B flat, where the opening figure is resumed at the end of the variations, without any sudden transition; and yet another, even more subtle, at the end of the third symphony, where the opening of the first movement reappears in notes lightly touched by the violins at the very end. The *Requiem* is not a mere collection of subtleties, whether technical or spiritual, for if it were nothing more than this, it would long ago have lost its power over mankind. It is the grandeur of its conception, the truth of the way in which it presents the essential truths of religion, the sincerity of its devotion, that give it its wonderful influence. It is true that the standard of vocal writing, both for solos and chorus, is of the highest, and that the orchestration is of the most masterly, having regard to Brahms's love of restraint and economy of material; but these are considerations that are willingly forgotten in the effect of the whole, and wherever it is adequately performed, the impression it produces on all thoughtful people—and on a good many who have not been accustomed to meditate on religious truths at all—is profound and indelible. To watch the congregation which fills St. Paul's Cathedral from end to end whenever Brahms's *Requiem* is given there, is to obtain the fullest refutation of the commonplace sneer that Brahms's music is for the few rather than for the many. Like every great thing in art, it was for the few at first; but for many years now it has been the property of the world at large.

The next work by Brahms in which a chorus is employed is Op. 50, the cantata *Rinaldo*, set to Goethe's poem, for male voices and orchestra with tenor solo. It is concerned only with the single episode of Rinaldo longing to stay on Armida's enchanted island, and being at last persuaded by his sailors to set sail, as the consequence of having been shown a shield of adamant. We are perhaps justified in considering that this piece represents pretty faithfully the style which Brahms would have adopted if he had found an operatic libretto to suit him; and if that is so, we may be very glad that that libretto was never found, for even if we dismiss from our minds all idea of comparisons with Wagner and modern dramatic music, the existing specimen has so many points of weakness in musical stage-craft that it is only too probable that an opera by Brahms would have shared the fate of Schumann's *Genoveva*, and after a few repetitions of a *succès d'estime*, would have been forgotten by every one except some very young and very fervent admirers. Of course, we must remember that it was never intended for the stage, and that therefore stagecraft was not called for; still, the one "situation" is treated in a more or less theatrical way, though it is calculated to convince no one. The conduct of the scene is handled with curious uncertainty. In this particular mood, there are numerous passages in Bruch's *Odysseus* that far exceed *Rinaldo* in the impression they produce. But at the same time, a master like Brahms could not put his name to a work of such magnitude unless it contained fine things; and when all is said, there remain parts of it that are worthy of the composer of the *Magelone-Lieder*, of certain of which the sea-music must remind us. The vigorous opening chorus, the voluptuous tenor solo, with its lovely slow movement, "Stelle hier der goldnen Tage," and the final chorus are effective, though the work as a whole can never meet with a very wide circle of admirers.

In the next two works requiring chorus, Opp. 53 and 54, Brahms again reflects upon the contrasts that inspired the most beautiful things in the *Requiem*—the contrasts, that is, between short-sighted views of human life and the serenity of the eternal verities. In the *Harzreise im Winter*, Goethe describes the character of a young man who was driven into melancholy by reading *Werther's Leiden*. It may be hard for us in the twentieth century to realize what an influence that romance had on impressionable Germans at the time it was written, but we know as a fact that it was very great. The victim of this melancholia, it is pleasant to know, recovered his mental balance, but not before he had inspired the poet with the beautiful fragment which, under the name of *Rhapsodie*, was set to music by Brahms for alto solo, male choir, and orchestra. The figure of the wanderer in dark woods groping his

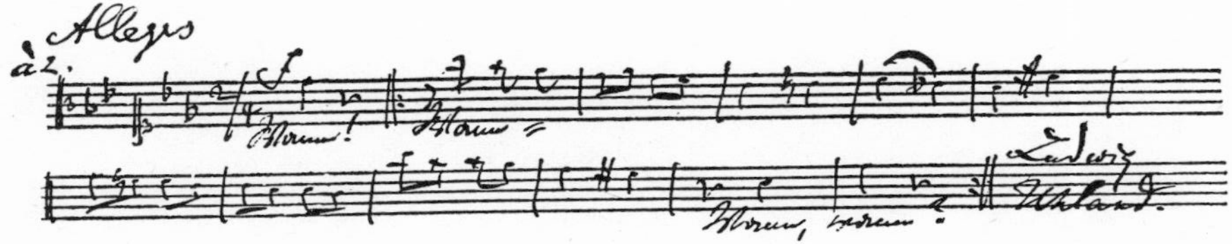

AUTOGRAPH CANON BY BRAHMS, FROM J. A. FULLER-MAITLAND'S "MASTERS OF GERMAN MUSIC" (1894), INSERTED THERE BY PERMISSION OF THE COMPOSER, AND OF G. MILNER-GIBSON-CULLUM, ESQ., THE OWNER OF THE ORIGINAL

way with incurable pain at his heart is painted for us by the soloist in a movement of uncertainty and misgiving. At the entry of a rhythm marked $\frac{6}{4}$, but wavering constantly between $\frac{3}{2}$ and $\frac{6}{4}$ in its arrangement of accents, we learn how, "from the fulness of love," the youth "drank but the hate of men"; and soon the original tempo is resumed, and the choir enters supporting the solo voice in the prayer, "If from Thy psalter, Father of Love, one note may reach his ear, let it refresh his heart; open his clouded sight to the thousand springs around him in the desert." The exquisitely flowing melody of this prayer is the perfect counterpart to what has gone before, and the colouring produced by the alto voice above the four-part male choir, and by the swaying figure of accompaniment in which there is generally one instrument playing triplets against the pairs of quavers in the others, make the work, short as it is, one of the most moving things in modern music. It was a singular whim of the composer's to speak of the *Rhapsodie* as if it were intended to be a kind of epilogue to the first *Liebeslieder*.[1]

In Op. 54, a setting for chorus and orchestra of Hölderlin's *Schicksalslied*, the contrast is drawn between the happy peace of heaven and the turmoil in which men live out their lives, dashed like the spray of a waterfall from one rock to another, finding rest nowhere, and ending in the abyss of uncertainty. The opening prelude is of truly celestial beauty, and the chorus continues the idea of beatific serenity. The rapid section in triple time, with many effects of crossing rhythms, such as Brahms always loved, suggests that the human race is driven about at random, like the dust by the wayside, and with the words "ins Ungewisse hinab" the poem ends. The poem, but

[1] See Kalbeck, ii. 298, 299.

not the music, for Brahms was too good a designer to let his work stop here, as well as having more confidence in a future life than the poet expressed. He resumes the movement of the opening part, for instruments alone, and sends us away with the idea of peace "beyond these voices." This merely instrumental close was itself an afterthought, for as at first projected the work was to have ended with a repetition of the opening words. Kalbeck, in his *Life*, ii. 365, gives the original ending in fascimile. The vocal and instrumental parts of this composition are equally happy in inspiration and in treatment, and the atmosphere of both sections is represented with wonderful fidelity.[1]

Though the *Schicksalslied* stands next in order of opus-numbers, it is separated from the *Rhapsodie* by the whole of the stirring events of the Franco-Prussian War, and although the composer was not directly concerned in them, seeing that he was a resident at Vienna at the time, yet his sympathy with his countrymen could not but find expression in the glorious *Triumphlied*, the "Hallelujah" from which was performed in Bremen Cathedral on Good Friday, 7 April, 1871, at a service in memory of those who had fallen in the war. The complete work was first given by the Philharmonic Society of Carlsruhe on 5 June, 1872. It is set for baritone solo, eight-part chorus, and orchestra. It is by no means an "occasional" piece, in the sense that its use in other circumstances than the original would involve some loss of appropriateness, and it is difficult to assign a reason for its infrequent performance at English festivals, where the north-country choirs would have such a splendid chance of showing themselves off. There is possibly a

[1] See the *Correspondence with Reinthaler*, 40, 42.

reason for its sedulous neglect in England,[1] in the very great difficulty of the vocal parts, and the strain upon the two soprano voices; but it may be guessed that another cause of its want of popularity here in England may be the fact that its first section is built on the theme of our own *God save the King*, which was appropriated as the German national anthem in 1790. English audiences unacquainted with the historical facts, and constitutionally reluctant to think that anything good in music can be of English origin, are easily induced to believe that we adopted our national anthem from Germany, instead of the reverse being the case. However this may be, the work is one which sorely needs frequent revival, for it is a noble song of victory, and among other things it reveals a spirit of grave exultation and thankfulness to God, which is a salutary corrective to certain forms of popular elation which have occasionally been seen in England. The whole of the first section is treated with the utmost elaboration, and the thematic material of the national anthem is never far away at any moment. A section in triple time, "Lobet unsern Gott," is not less imposing, and in its course an outburst of "Hallelujahs" (and the resumption of common time) leads to what has been called the "proclamation"—"Denn der allmächtige Gott hat das Reich eingenommen"—in which the voices are used in close imitation. This portion gives way in turn to a passage in which the second choir sings in $\frac{12}{8}$ time, and the whole is built on the strains of the hymn, *Nun danket alle Gott.* The third and last section carries us back to the *Requiem*, by

[1] Since the above was written, performances of the *Triumphlied* have been given by the Handel Society and the Royal Choral Society.

its use of a baritone solo to announce the apocalyptic vision of the rider on the white horse, and we seem to hear and see the new empire being founded on truth and justice. For a brief space our attention is turned to Him who "treads the winepress of the wrath of God," and a great climax is reached at the point where the soloist announces the Name that is written on the conqueror's vesture and on His thigh, the words "King of kings, and Lord of lords" being uttered, not by the soloist, but by the basses of the first choir, with magnificent effect of grandeur. On the theme of this phrase is built the jubilant chorus which follows and ends the work.

After these important choral works, the seven unaccompanied songs, Op. 62, must seem rather slight. The first, *Rosmarin*, is a delicious little "volksthümliches Lied" for choir; the second, *Von alten Liebesliedern*, has an attractive rhythm of three bars, twice over, and then a five-bar phrase; as both the male and female parts are occasionally divided it is only theoretically in four parts. *Waldesnacht* and *Dein Herzlein mild* are of the simplest structure and most winning charm. *All' meine Herzgedanken* is in six parts, and is one of the few compositions of Brahms which might almost be called a madrigal in the strict sense. *Es geht ein Wehen*, in five parts, has an uncanny ambiguity, as the basses reiterate a third of the minor key in such a way as to suggest at first that it is the tonic of the major. *Vergangen ist mir Glück und Heil*, the last of the set, had already appeared as a solo in Op. 48, where its accompaniment is so strictly in four parts that a mere transference to the voices was all that was needed to make it a most beautiful and impressive part-song. Its use of the Dorian mode is such as would satisfy any but the most pedantic of modal theorists.

The next choral works are separated from these by many sets of songs and by the first two symphonies, and their austere style contrasts strangely with the charming grace of the second symphony, which immediately preceded them in publication. Op. 74 consists of two motets for mixed choir unaccompanied, each in several movements. The first, *Warum ist das Licht*, is set to words which are perhaps "heathenish" in the sense in which Brahms used that word to Frau von Herzogenberg,[1] but the manner in which the mood passes from doubt and gloom to the confident note which distinguishes the chorale, *Mit Fried' und Freud' ich fahr' dahin*, is worthy of some of the best of Bach's church cantatas, and the words are a noble sermon in themselves. We are not told if any one put them together for Brahms, and it is surely allowable to suppose that for a theme so congenial to him through his life he was indebted to no one. The opening words are an almost exact prophecy of the four *Serious Songs*, and the longing for death expressed by the miserable was an idea that must have appealed strongly to Brahms at all times. The repeated question, "Warum?" makes a kind of natural division between three subsections of the first number, the first being fugal, the second giving a vivid picture of those who wait in vain for death, and the third starting with a striking unison passage, "Und dem Manne, dess Weg verborgen ist," in triple time. The second movement, in six parts, has a beautiful phrase suggesting the idea of the uplifted heart of the worshipper. Yet it was not originally composed for these words, "Lasset uns unser Herz sammt den Händen aufheben," but was the theme of the *Benedictus* of the

[1] See p. 32.

early contrapuntal mass which has been referred to; the theme was found by Kalbeck in the one remaining part-book containing the music for the Hamburg Ladies' Choir.[1] The third movement, *Siehe, wir preisen selig*, again in six parts, is a glorious piece of full polyphony, but all too short, and it leads into another six-part section, *Die Geduld Hiob habt ihr gehöret*, in which there is an antiphonal effect at the beginning, and a remarkable resumption of the lovely close of the second section. The whole ends with a chorale, *Mit Fried' und Freud'*, treated after the manner of Bach, in four more or less florid parts. The second motet, *O Heiland, reiss' die Himmel auf*, is a chorale-cantata without solos; that is to say, each verse of the hymn is treated differently, the melody being predominant in each. In the first verse it is set in the soprano, with imitative passages in the others; a similar arrangement prevails in verse two, but the imitations are in a different shape and speed. In the third, the tune is in the tenor part, and in the fourth in the bass, the fifth being in the manner of a double fugue. There is a specially fine rolling "Amen" to close the motet. The theme is possibly taken from one of the regular German chorales, but it seems not to have been identified as yet, and may, after all, be Brahms's own. It is curious to find that, as Kalbeck states,[2] this second motet was written after, if not actually inspired by, the death of Hermann Goetz.

The next choral work, Op. 82, a setting of Schiller's *Nänie* for choir and orchestra, inspired by the death of Feuerbach the painter, is yet another meditation on the brevity of life, and the inevitable nature of death. The scoring is rich and the vocal writing exceedingly grateful to

[1] See pp. 16, 196, and Kalbeck, i. 386. [2] i. 398.

the singers. At the description of the rising of Thetis from the sea there is a fine change of tonality and style, the former movement is resumed after a time, and the composer's hopefulness appears in his repetition of the word "herrlich" at the close, though what Schiller calls "splendid" is nothing more exciting than the fate of becoming a lament in the mouth of a beloved friend. In connexion with this work it may be mentioned that in the days when it was new another setting of the same words by Hermann Goetz was enjoying a brief period of admiration, particularly in England; it is, indeed, one of Goetz's most happily inspired compositions, but the comparison between them, even granting that Goetz's is the better of the two, was rather a slight foundation on which to build an opinion that Brahms was inferior to him as a composer. Yet this opinion, absurd as it now seems, was held, not by a mere handful of irresponsible amateurs, but by certain musicians of earnest aim.

The setting of Goethe's *Gesang der Parzen* for six-part choir and orchestra, Op. 89, is inevitably thought of as a companion piece to *Nänie*, although two years elapsed between the publication of the one and of the other. The *Song of the Fates* begins antiphonally, the three male voices answering the three upper parts. The music is throughout austere, as befits the character of the poem, and there is a wonderfully mysterious passage at the words, "Im Finstern." Even in setting these sombre words, Brahms will not leave his hearers with unrelieved gloom in their hearts. "He seems," as Miss May says,[1] "in his setting of the last strophe but one to concentrate attention on the past kindness

[1] *Life of Brahms*, ii. 206.

of the gods, and thus, perhaps, subtly to suggest a plea for present hope."

Op. 93 consists of short choral works, the six songs without accompaniment being numbered 93*a*, and the *Tafellied*, which has a pianoforte accompaniment, standing by itself as Op. 93*b*. *Der bucklichte Fiedler* is a merry description of a village revel, with a touch of realism at the beginning of the waltz-section, where the voices imitate the tuning of the fiddle. *Das Mädchen* was afterwards published as a song, in Op. 95; in its first form it has a soprano solo above the four-part chorus, and its rhythm is an alternation of $\frac{3}{4}$ and common time, otherwise a rhythm of seven crotchets in the bar. *O süsser Mai!* is of slighter quality, and *Fahr' wohl!* though so short, is of unspeakable beauty, and the way its cadence leads to the repetition of the opening is particularly charming. *Der Falke* is, perhaps, less distinguished than this, but *Beherzigung* is a remarkably vigorous little piece in canon. The *Tafellied*, otherwise called *Dank der Damen*, is a light and gallant dialogue between the ladies and the gentlemen at a feast, and at the climax, at the words, "Recht so!" the six voices join together with excellent effect.

In Op. 104 we reach the culmination of Brahms's work as a writer for voices unaccompanied. The five songs of which it consists are one and all concerned with the transitory nature of human life, and from the first to the last are among the most individual compositions of their author. The first two are called *Nachtwache*, and are set to words by Rückert. *Leise Töne der Brust* opens in a dialogue between the upper and lower halves of the usual six-part division of the chorus. When delicately sung (and the whole effect of these songs is lost if a large choir attempts them) this plaintive thing passes over like a sigh; and in the next, *Ruh'n sie?* we breathe the very air of romance. The question, "Do they rest?" is passed on as though from one sentinel to another, in a phrase that falls from tonic to dominant; and the answer, "They rest!" comes back, passing from dominant to tonic. This composition was sung at the master's grave, in 1897. In *Letztes Glück* there is a close imitation between the upper and lower halves of the choir, and a cadence of exceptional beauty. *Verlorene Jugend* is in five parts, and is strophic in form, with a change from minor to major that brings no change of mood. The last, *Im Herbst*, is in four parts, and opens in C minor with the chord of the submediant, producing a momentary ambiguity as to key; at the third verse there is an intenser passion of regret, but the close is made in C major with beautiful effect. The set of songs, though naturally rather gloomy in tone, is of ineffable loveliness to those who can appreciate delicacy in choral writing and choral singing; but the big north-country choirs of England may be advised not to attempt them. A small band of about twenty solo-singers is the ideal medium for their interpretation.

Op. 109, the next choral composition, consists of three eight-part choruses entitled *Fest- und Gedenksprüche*, and dedicated to the Burgomaster of Brahms's native city, Hamburg; they were performed there at the first of three festival concerts arranged by Bülow for the opening of the Hamburg Industrial Exhibition of 1889. They were a practical acknowledgment of the honour which his native place had conferred upon him in the "freedom of the city." In the first, *Unsere Väter hofften auf Dich*, a solemn and jubilant passage for the second choir in broad unisonous phrases is answered by florid ornamentation in the first choir; soon the fabric is more closely knit, and the powerful close is very broad. The second, *Wenn ein starker Gewappneter*, has a more rapid interchange of dialogue between the two choruses, and is marked throughout by appropriate vigour and dignity. The third, *Wo ist ein so herrlich Volk*, points out the lesson of God's providence, and warns the hearers against confidence in themselves. There is a fine and solemn passage of the utmost breadth and bigness at the words "Hüte dich nur," and the "Amen" resumes the theme of the opening.

The group of three motets, published immediately after these as Op. 110, begins with an eight-part work, *Ich aber bin elend*, with an opening of remarkable impressiveness; at the words "Herr, herr Gott!" one choir whispers the consoling words "Barmherzig und gnädig und geduldig," while the other repeats the three chords of the opening invocation. The second, in four parts, *Ach, arme Welt!* is, like the other, gloomy in character, and this is increased by the introduction of a D natural into the key of F minor, producing a suggestion of the severe Dorian mode. The third, *Wenn wir im höchsten Nöthen sein*, is very austere and difficult even for the most accomplished singers.

In his last work for chorus Brahms returns to his old love, folk-song, and although Op. 113 is called by the forbidding name of "Canons," nothing more dreadful is meant than what we in England call "rounds." They are thirteen in number, and many are of "volksthümlich" character, if not actual fragments of traditional melody. Several of them date from the old days when Brahms and Joachim exchanged their contrapuntal compositions. The first and second are to words of Goethe; all are for female voices, some requiring a very large compass. The four-part *Sitzt a schön's Vögerl* is on a charming three-bar tune, and the three-part *Schlaf! Kindlein, schlaf!* is deliciously caressing; *Wille, wille, will* is very humorous; these three had appeared as single songs in the early collection of *Volkskinderlieder.* In No. 6, *So lange Schönheit wird bestehn,* there is a more elaborate canonic treatment than the strict unisonous imitation followed hitherto. The two sopranos have the canon in the ordinary way, the two altos inverting the same subject. Another double canon is No. 9, in which the pair of parts sung by the sopranos is imitated exactly a fifth below by the two altos. No. 10 is a setting of Rückert's *Leise Töne der Brust* (see Op. 104, No. 1), and the next three are in the plaintive mood we connect with Brahms's later years, so far as his vocal music is concerned. No. 13 is a four-part canon for soprano voices supported by what is technically called a *pes* on the tonic and dominant of the key, alternating in the two alto voices and making a kind of "drone." This drone-bass is necessary, for the little piece *Einförmig ist der Liebe Gram* is but an adaptation of the famous *Leyermann* of Schubert; and there is something very suggestive and pathetic in the idea that Brahms should have finished his career as a choral writer by a reference to his great Viennese predecessor. Schubert's last song from the *Winterreise* has struck many people as applying with singularly pathetic force to his own case; and though Brahms can never have felt, for many years before his death, that his own "kleiner Teller bleibt ihm immer leer," yet in the melancholy mood produced by his illness he may well have felt even his hopefulness of disposition forsaking him, and have been haunted by the plaintive little song of Schubert, so that he arranged it in this new form.

We have traced the development of Brahms's art from the earliest pianoforte sonata, through all the classes of music which he adorned with his genius. It is difficult to know where to consider that the end of his work and of his career came; there were happily many important works both vocal and instrumental, to come after these canons that mark the end of his choral music; most notable of all, of course, are the four *Ernste Gesänge* which close the list of his published works; but the single posthumous work, the set of chorale-preludes for organ, is perhaps to be regarded even more definitely as the close of his labours, and their conclusion is even more appropriate, as showing unmistakably the humble confidence with which his soul betook itself to rest. Of Brahms it is true, as of so very few among the popular musicians of their day, that "He being dead, yet speaketh"; and as the years flow on since his death, notwithstanding all the changes of musical fashion that have passed over the world in general, the message of hope, of manly endeavour, of trust in a higher power, and of assured conviction of the truth of the artistic principles he obeyed, must ever grow more and more strongly and be more widely listened to. This is not music that time can age; like Bach's, it must be more and more widely understood and loved as time goes on; and more and more universal must be the world's acceptance of Brahms as one of the supreme masters among the composers of all time.

LIST OF THE COMPOSITIONS OF BRAHMS

LIST OF THE COMPOSITIONS OF BRAHMS, ARRANGED IN ORDER OF OPUS-NUMBERS

The excellent *Thematisches Verzeichniss* published by Simrock & Co. may be recommended to readers who wish for more detailed information. The figures in the last column refer to the pages of this book on which the works are mentioned. Dates of publication are added in brackets.

COMPOSITIONS

OPUS		PAGES
1.	Sonata in C major for pianoforte solo (1853)	8, 66, 75, 81, 83, 85, 196
2.	Sonata in F sharp minor for pianoforte solo (1853) ...	72, 75, 81, 83, 85, 86, 193, 196
3.	Six Songs. Liebestreu, Liebe und Frühling (1 and 2), Weit über das Feld, In der Fremde, and Lindes Rauschen (1854)	6, 161, 162, 196
4.	Scherzo in E flat minor for pianoforte solo (1854) ...	6, 9, 75, 81, 86, 87
5.	Sonata in F minor for pianoforte solo (1854)	71, 72, 75, 81, 83, 87, 88, 125, 196
6.	Six Songs. Spanisches Lied, Der Frühling, Nachwirkung, Juchhe! Wie die Wolke, Nachtigallen schwingen (1853)	162, 163
7.	Six Songs. Treue Liebe, Parole, Anklänge, Volkslied, Die Trauernde, Heimkehr (1854)	161, 163
8.	Trio for piano and strings in B major (1854)	75, 76, 100, 107, 108, 196
9.	Variations for pianoforte solo on a theme of Schumann (1854)	9, 88, 89
10.	Four Balladen for pianoforte solo (1856)	9, 54, 67, 76, 89, 90, 193
11.	Serenade in D major for orchestra (1860)	76, 131, 147, 196
12.	Ave Maria for female choir and orchestra (1861)	16, 17, 196, 20

OPUS		PAGES
93*b*.	Tafellied (Dank der Damen) for six-part choir with pianoforte accompaniment (1885)	216
94.	Five Songs. Mit vierzig Jahren, Steig' auf, geliebte Schatten, Mein Herz ist schwer, Sapphische Ode, Kein Haus, keine Heimath (1884)	68, 181, 182
95.	Seven Songs. Das Mädchen ("Stand das Mädchen"), Bei dir sind meine Gedanken, Beim Abschied, Der Jäger, Vorschneller Schwur, Mädchenlied ("Am jüngsten Tag"), Schön war, das ich dir weihte (1884)	62, 182, 216
96.	Four Songs. Der Tod, das ist die kühle Nacht, Wir wandelten, Es schauen die Blumen, Meerfahrt (1886)	182, 183
97.	Six Songs. Nachtigall, Auf dem Schiffe, Entführung, Dort in den Weiden, Komm' bald, Trennung (1886)	183
98.	Symphony in E minor, No. 4 (1886)	28, 79, 152–5, 183
99.	Sonata in F major for pianoforte and violoncello (1887)	123, 183
100.	Sonata in A major for pianoforte and violin (1887) ...	71, 98, 123, 184
101.	Trio in C minor for pianoforte and strings (1887) ...	122, 124
102.	Concerto in A minor for violin and violoncello (1888) ...	49, 79, 155, 156, 183
103.	Zigeunerlieder, eleven gipsy songs for vocal quartet and piano (1888). (Eight of them arranged for solo voice, 1889)	74, 184, 195
104.	Five Part-songs for unaccompanied chorus. Nachtwache (1 and 2), Letztes Glück, Verlorene Jugend, Im Herbst (1889)	79, 216, 217
105.	Five Songs. Wie Melodien, Immer leiser, Klage, Auf dem Kirchhofe, Verrath (1889)	80, 95, 123, 183, 184
106.	Five Songs. Ständchen, Auf dem See, Es hing der Reif, Meine Lieder, Ein Wanderer (1889)	183, 185
107.	Five Songs. An die Stolze, Salamander, Das Mädchen spricht, Maienkätzchen, Mädchenlied (1889)... ...	183, 185
108.	Sonata in D minor for pianoforte and violin (1889) ...	71, 124, 125
109.	Fest- und Gedenksprüche for eight-part choir unaccompanied. Unsere Väter, Wenn ein starker Gewappneter, Wo ist ein so herrlich Volk (1890)	217, 218
110.	Three Motets for four- and eight-part choir unaccompanied. Ich aber bin elend, Ach, arme Welt, Wenn wir in höchsten Nöthen sein (1890)	218
111.	Quintet in G major for strings (1891)	68, 122, 125, 126

WORKS WITHOUT OPUS-NUMBERS

ARRANGEMENTS, ETC.

EARLY WORKS (not now known to exist)

LIST OF FIRST LINES AND TITLES OF VOCAL COMPOSITIONS

LIST OF FIRST LINES AND TITLES OF VOCAL COMPOSITIONS

In the following list the convenient register at the end of the *Thematisches Verzeichniss* published by Simrock has been used. Note that in a group of songs, the first line of each song is followed by the number of the pages on which the whole group, or any part of it, is referred to. Thus, under the separate titles of each of the *Magelone-Lieder*, the pages on which reference is made to the whole set of these songs are given. The titles of the songs are printed in Italic, the opening words in Roman type. "Volksl." without a date after it, refers to the seven books of *Deutsche Volkslieder* published in 1894.

INDEX

INDEX